Acknowledgments & Dedication

Dedicated to the spiritual growth of each individual Christian and to the opening of each unbeliever's heart; to the inadequacies of written words in expressing the depth and breadth of God's love for us, and to the example He has given to us through His Son Christ Jesus as to how we are to love others selflessly and unconditionally.

To my brothers and sisters, to Mom, to my children for their patience during the writing of this book and The Torn Veil, as well as to their future spiritual growth; to Patti, Faye and my extended family. To my spiritual mentors including Bob George, Pastor Jim Woods, Pastor Earnest Thompson, Pastor Bruce Dick and Pastor Lee Nunemaker. To all who have helped me through the years to better understand God's grace message. To Doris and to the entire Landis family and especially to my great friend Daniel Landis who will always live in our hearts.

"Did you respond to the God who rewards good works and righteous deeds based on your own worldly definition of love; or to the God who justifies those who fall short of His glory because of their sin nature, and to Christ's example of how we are to love others in agape love?"

Daniel Landis

Seasons Of Grace Perfection

Table Of Contents

Chapter 1   The Law Pointing Towards Grace

Chapter 2   Foundations of Biblical Salvation

Chapter 3   The Permanence of Salvation

Chapter 4   The Grace Message

Chapter 5   Death of Our Human Desires & Sin Nature

Chapter 6   The Spiritual Nature and Grief

Chapter 7   Prayer

Chapter 8   The Anointed Cherub and Worldliness

Preface

Prior to my Christian salvation in 1992, I spent many years searching to understand God's truth by following those who I thought understood spiritual truths greater than I, reading the Bible, listening intently to church speakers, engaging in prayer, talking to many people in all walks of life, attending Bible studies and living my life according to what I intuitively thought was consistent with being a Christian. Often, my actions were seemingly noble, but misguided. With this, I was able to learn much about the truth in God's word by understanding a great deal as to what it was not. By the time of my salvation, I had accumulated a tremendous amount of knowledge based all on what the Holy Spirit was teaching me. In many cases, this involved a process of unlearning many things I had been taught in Christian circles throughout my life. I continued for another ten years after my salvation to immerse myself in God's word and learn as much as I could, anywhere I could, through watching and listening to others and trying to practice my faith. I was unwilling to accept other people's views on key topics in the Bible without first questioning and verifying what they were telling me in Scripture. This, combined with 30 years of indoctrination in the past by ceremonial based and often legalistic churches I attended, gave me a greater conviction and purpose to allow the Holy Spirit to be my final teacher when there were so many inconsistencies which surrounded me.

The result of those years was the writing and publishing of *The Torn Veil: An Invitation and Commentary To The Christian Life*. It was the accumulation of what I had learned through time and my research, both head and heart knowledge, and was intended to be an exhaustive reference book on many important topic areas. Each chapter reflected my search and struggles to reconcile the inconsistencies of that which I had learned through my life, with many things I was learning for the first time in the Bible. The chapters of *The Torn Veil* provided answers to the many questions I had on God's word, many of which I was able to use as excuses (prior to my salvation) to maintain and hold onto carnal control of my life and prevent me from submitting to salvation through Christ. Each chapter in *The Torn Veil* reflected the many spiritual, intellectual, and emotionally charged questions I had prior to my salvation; questions that had to be answered to the satisfaction of my logical carnal nature and world view mindset before I could ever fully submit to accepting the free gift that was part of the New Covenant I was learning about in the Bible. The topics were fascinating and exciting and included the inconsistencies of so many Christian religions contrasted with Biblical truths, creationism and evolution, contradictions, and confusing issues in the Bible, the seemingly unfairness of God's word, Christian salvation being temporary or permanent, the use of alcohol by the Christian, celebrations of holidays, the contrasts between the Old Covenant and New, and many others. In the end, and prior to my salvation, I realized my carnal and worldly understanding could only take me so far in the journey God had prepared for me in my spiritual walk.

The Torn Veil provided me a foundation to understand multiple areas that were confusing to me and how God was challenging me in all areas of my life. I realized, and felt strongly, that each Christian has their own book or story to write which consists of all aspects of their personal relationship with the Lord and their Christian walk. Essentially, an accounting of the circumstances that led up to their salvation, their early struggles, what God was currently doing in their lives, the obstacles they were overcoming in their spiritual lives, how they were influencing others, and the conclusions they arrived at in the many areas of what God's word was challenging them to understand and apply. As Christians, each of us has a unique and special personal relationship with the Lord. The collection of experiences we have in this world as well as the awareness God gives us based in knowledge and in our hearts, all combine to make up a journal of spiritual struggles, growth, and amazing fulfillment in the tremendous life's journey that God gives each of us.

One of the major themes of *The Torn Veil* was that under the New Covenant God establishes with us, we can tear back the (Old Covenant) veil of legalism and religious structure based on guilt, punitive approaches and human controls which bind and limit us in so many ways. We can approach God without any human interpreter or religious system to inhibit that intimate personal relationship and understanding, and therefore establish full spiritual personal accountability.

The sequel to *The Torn Veil*, *Seasons Of Grace Perfection*, was written with three purposes: To challenge believers to fully understand the amazing freedom they have in their salvation and with that freedom and through grace, to demonstrate the same level of responsibility in using their gifts and talents to God's glory based on the high expectations He has for us in the New Covenant; as a manifestation of the Holy Spirit which indwells in us. This is all based on our unique personal relationship we have in Christ as the Holy Spirit guides us; a relationship which is defined by our own gifts, our special calling, the challenges each of us have that are the same and simultaneously, those that are different. Secondly, *Seasons* was written to clearly articulate the concept of "The Grace Message" and to put into words key dynamics of this amazing collection of God's creation; what God's grace actually means, what it does not mean, and how it is different from the law. Thirdly, *Seasons* was written to open the hearts of unbelievers to amazing and joyous Biblical truths and to God's love for us.

Seasons Of Grace Perfection looks at the practical aspects of our struggles with our sin nature and outlines foundational truths of our relationship with God. In this context, it is not God's grace to us that moves towards perfection. Instead, it is our Christian walk with God as we show love towards others, and as we grow in grace through the many joyful and challenging seasons of our lives. This growth moves us more towards spiritual perfection on this earth as we make choices to follow the leading of the Holy Spirit who guides us throughout our lifelong process of becoming progressively sanctified. Through all the seasons of our lives, we move forward and take steps in our spiritual growth journey, and we make mistakes that we learn from through humble self-introspection, interactions with others, a desire to improve and let old things pass away; all which occurs underneath God's sovereign umbrella as part of His wonderful and magnificent creation. We can understand something intellectually and not necessarily grasp it emotionally, to the full depth that it needs to be understood. In this context, our arena of our growth takes place in four areas: spiritual, intellectual, emotional, and physical. Each of these is inextricably connected to the others.

In their book *Leadership Agility*, Joiner and Josephs refer to growth in a leader as "Developmental Motivation". An example of this is I say something in a business meeting. As I am driving out of the parking lot that evening to go home, I reflect and realize I may have come across to that person as being too abrasive. The next day, I go to that person and apologize. The next time I'm in a meeting, I say something again that may be abrasive, but I immediately catch myself and apologize to that person, and then rephrase it a different way. The next time I'm in a meeting and I am tempted to say something abrasive, and based on my motivation to develop and grow, I hold back from saying anything at all until I have reflected, carefully formulated my words, and then share them in the meeting. This example aligns well with the Biblical principle that, as we grow, "old things that are from the sin nature pass away".

Introduction

God created us as free moral agents with the freedom to choose Him or the sin of this world. He was and is willing to let us make a free choice, a choice which can result in us not including His spiritual presence for eternity and therefore depriving Him of having each of us as His child in Heaven. From Him, this is all for the sake of respecting our dignity and right to choose as free agents. So that we could have a free life according to how we would define it, He gave up His control of us by allowing us to freely choose Him, or this world. As believers, we understand the greatest life we can have is that which we can live in Christ, through the Holy Spirit living in us.

Seasons Of Grace Perfection examines the many wonderful aspects of grace and how our relationship with others is tied to how we comprehend and experience grace from God. Circumstances that God gives to us in each of our lives reveal important parts of our character for us to see; parts of our character we would not otherwise see unless God revealed them to us through life's many circumstances. As we look back in our lives in retrospect, we can see that the condition and dynamics of our character was always there, but we could not see it until it was illuminated in some way against the backdrop of something that would later put it into context. Once we become aware of these aspects of our character that need work, we then have the choice as well as the spiritual responsibility to act and do something about them. This includes not only a change of heart and intent (that is internal and something others may not be able to see) but also a change in outward action. Paul tells us in Philippians 1:6 that he is certain that with our salvation, God has begun a good work in us and will perfect it until Jesus returns. As we grow in grace, this good work continues and progresses.

There are examples of this with the four seasons in nature where conditions make it much easier to see things that, without them, would be impossible to see. As we look at the effects of wind for example and after corn has been harvested in the summer, all that is left in the fields are very small pieces of corn stalks and leaves on the ground. In the heat of the day, the small cornstalk particles and leaves dry out and become very light. When the wind blows, it's very easy to see visual patterns because these corn particles move so easily from the effects of the wind. Often, I have seen dust devils and very small tornadoes in these fields, which I never would have been able to see unless the conditions were there to illuminate them; the conditions being the small dried out corn stalk particles and the dust devils. This same effect with the wind occurs in all other seasons as well. In the winter with very light powdery snow, these dust devils can be seen only because of the light snow on the ground. If the light snow was not present, the subtle circular movement of the wind could not be seen. In autumn, when small leaves fall off trees and then dry out, dust devils occur and can be seen only because of these leaves illuminating the wind. In spring, small seeds on the ground are lifted and swirled about in circular motions with the results of the wind seen only because of the presence of these light seeds. In all these examples involving dust devils and mini tornadoes, the wind was moving in a circular motion. If the corn particles, snow powder, leaves or seeds were not there, the wind still would have been producing small tornadoes, but in no way could be seen.

In much the same way and throughout our lives, there are things about our character that are ever present (analogous to the corn pieces, snow powder, small leaves and seeds), but we are unable to see them until God provides peripheral conditions (wind and dust devils) where they are illuminated against a backdrop where we can better see and understand them. When this occurs, we become aware of them and can see with perfect clarity the extent of God's blessings to us but also certain opportunities for growth in our character. What we do with this self-awareness and new knowledge is up to us. Hebrews 5:13-6:1 tells us that, as we grow in grace, God gives us things that are more and more challenging to us based on our spiritual maturity and how much we are willing to be receptive and open to learning about continuing in our strengths and leveraging opportunities for improvement through our weaknesses. With this, He knows when we are most able to understand and appreciate things, we can learn about ourselves. All of us have had the experience of understanding for the first time the real meaning of a Biblical verse or concept which we had read or experienced numerous times before. God knew we were not yet spiritually mature enough or ready to understand it prior to that moment; like how a parent guides and observes one of their children.

At the time of our salvation, (covered more in depth in Chapter 1), we become righteous in the eyes of God and in an important context, become spiritually perfect in His eyes. As God gives us circumstances, and as we grow in grace within the many seasons of our lives, as in the many seasons of nature, we become more and more sanctified, more aware as to the depths of His blessings to us and closer to His expectation for the amazing contributions through love we can make in this world guided by the Holy Spirit which lives in us. This is God's purpose for us, to use the gifts He has given to us to experience His amazing love more fully and to share that with others so they may experience that love, freedom, grace and opportunity.

As we grow in grace throughout our Christian walk, and although our identity in Christ does not change, we go through many different seasons of our lives where God is working on us like a potter to His clay, molding us towards the person He wants us to be through a sanctification process. We go through many seasons where the grace and love we show to others moves more and more towards the spiritual perfection God wants for us as we struggle with the sin nature that will always be in us on this earth.

We are surrounded by a culture which places tremendous value and worth on our efforts, actions, works, deeds, accomplishments, and behaviors which, all too often, "define" our success or outlines our character or identity in the eyes of others. Examples of this include the world of sports, academics, capitalism itself and competition for scarce resources on so many fronts. Because of this, intuitively we tend to believe that religion and our spiritual life should be based on these same efforts, works and deeds. Our standing with God however (and as clearly outlined in the Bible), is never determined by our works and what we have done to earn salvation or to maintain it.

As Christians, we must not only deal with the humanistic world views which surround us but unfortunately, with the overwhelming influence of false doctrines and apostasy from well intentioned (and sometimes not so well intentioned) but misguided Christians. Sometimes, these distortions are severe and evil. In our efforts to share the gospel of love and grace to others, and as we model the way guided by the Holy Spirit which indwells in us, often we first have to undue damage already inflicted by Christians whose doctrines are based on legalism or, to the other extreme, an over emphasis on liberalistic "anything goes" Christianity. Each of us is challenged to find things out for ourselves, to "study to show ourselves approved" and as the Bereans did, examine doctrines, scriptures and all that surrounds us in the context of how the Holy Spirit guides that interpretation, always being aware that our sin nature prefers us to discern those same things according to our carnal worldly desires which satisfy us for the short term, but leave us empty through eternity. This difficulty to experience God's word and His perfect will for our lives is also compounded by traditions we have come to fully accept which may be incorrect and/or doctrines that we have been taught since childhood which must be challenged and proof tested.

In the first year of marriage, I came to fully realize the degree to which our spiritual viewpoints were different, although both of us had come from legalistic works-based churches. After several months and some real soul searching, the truth became apparent to me that I wasn't sure how I felt about many issues relating to Christianity; especially salvation. Out of fear and a desire to have more confidence as to how I believed we should raise our children once they came along, I began the process of going through the Bible feverishly looking for versus which supported the viewpoints I had accepted my whole life. Any verse that I read which in any way contradicted my current long held existing beliefs were quickly dismissed and rejected. I was not at all concerned with the objective truth but was instead focused on maintaining (and protecting) my firmly held rigid beliefs out of insecurity. This was all orchestrated so that I would not have to change my viewpoints and give up that which I had believed ever since I could remember. As time went by, the Holy Spirit convicted me as to what God's truth was and as this happened, many of the viewpoints and beliefs I held onto so intensely began to be rejected and let go of.

Seasons Of Grace Perfection is written to examine the spiritual relationship each of us has with God which is like all other believers' but yet simultaneously, completely unique from all others with individualistic standards and challenges God gives to us. It is an amazing and extremely powerful blessing that God gives us different seasons in our lives to become more aware of things, to grow, to break down, to build up, to cast away stones, to gather them up, to cry, to celebrate, to cherish wonderful times and to let some go, to experience great joy, to join together, to be thankful, to show grace, and to love.

George Elliot once said: "It's never too late to be what you might have been." There is nothing we can do about the past and time that has gone by. There is much we can do about the present and the future that awaits each of us, and to live into God's potential for us. We each have been created as free agents with tremendous gifts, talents, capacities and callings. We are empowered to make our own deliberate and intentional choices to influence this world, and those in it who are put in front of us, according to our spiritual, emotional, intellectual, and physical blessings. As we go through the different seasons of our lives and our own unique process of Christian sanctification where we progressively are more able to allow the Holy Spirit to freely work through us unencumbered by our carnal worldly selves, our capacity to demonstrate grace is slowly perfected. Essentially, a journey through our own personal and spiritual collection of all the seasons of our grace perfection; all as we journey to demonstrate love according to the principles in I Corinthians 13 and the fruits of the Spirit in Galatians 5 and 6.

Chapter 1

The Law Pointing Towards Grace

In the book of Genesis, God's expectation of Adam and Eve was for them to tend the Garden of Eden in a perfect and pure relationship in His creation. Adam was placed in a perfect utopian world and the only mandate he had from God was to not eat from the Tree of Knowledge of good and evil. He was permitted to eat from the Tree of Life however but chose not to exercise that privilege. We can only wonder what this world would have been like had Adam eaten only from the Tree of Life. God told Adam that if he ate from the Tree of Knowledge (Genesis 2:17), he would die spiritually. Genesis 3:1 tells us that God made the serpent, along with all the other creatures He created (Genesis 1:20-25), and that the serpent was more cunning than any of the other creatures that He made. To God's glory and credit, He gave Adam and Eve the ability to make free choices in the Garden (as He does so for us today). If He had not, Adam and Eve never would have been able to choose to disobey Him; or conversely, to choose to obey Him, as was God's perfect will for them. Adam and Eve chose to disobey God's only desire because they were tempted by Satan. The serpent was able to convince Eve that both she and Adam would be like God if they ate from the Tree of Knowledge; and so they did.

Because of Adam's decision to disobey God, mankind's sin nature was **"activated"** for all time so that all men and women (born after Adam and Eve) would be born with a sin nature. I use the word "activated" here because Adam was created with the ability to choose to obey God, or to disobey Him. With that ability to choose for or against God, came his ability to choose things consistent with the spirit nature or consistent with a sin nature. The sin nature which exists inside each of us provides the option for each of us to sin. James 1:13 tells us that God does not tempt anyone but does give us the choice (as free moral agents) to decide what we will choose, the things of the sin nature or the things of the spiritual nature. The only way Adam and Eve then could have sinned against God in the Garden was if they were driven by their sin nature to respond inappropriately to any temptation from Satan. Committing a sin (in this context) would consist of not only having a sin nature, which would make being able to sin within the realm of possibilities for behaviors, but simultaneously, there existing some temptation where that sin nature would be activated to sin and where someone would want to make the choice to give into that sin nature.

God created Adam and Eve not only with the desire to want to please Him and live in perfect harmony but also with the ability to choose to go against His will. Adam sinned and went against God because he chose to give into his sin nature. When God created Adam and Eve, He gave them the freedom to make choices. If they decided to make choices that were consistent with God's perfect will, their decisions would be glorifying God. If they chose to make decisions that were inconsistent with and disobedient to God's will for them, they would then be employing their sin nature. Along with this sin nature, God gave them the responsibility to accept and live with the results of these choices whether they would be in the form of blessings, or negative consequences.

In the Old Covenant, the Ten Commandments were given to Moses by God for all mankind with the expectation for us to live by the law. This was because of Adam's fall. Under its system, sin and its consequences were each person's master. In the Old Covenant, our relationship with God was determined by the extent to which we were able to overcome the temptation of sin and keep the law. The law required that each individual produces perfect acts of good based on self-effort, good deeds, and works. The law of the Old Covenant, however, was given by God to show us that we, through our own works, could not be perfect in the His eyes. The law, as part of God's plan, pointed us to grace (which would be found only in the New Covenant) because of our inability to keep that law; a law that we, in a true manner of speaking, had requested from God based on our own contrived method as to how we believed we should be eligible to enter God's perfect Heaven based on our carnal perspective. Under the Old Covenant law, if a person violated one part of the law, he/she was said to have violated the entire law. This was a requirement of this system of law. It galvanized man's inabilities to live righteously in God's eyes by saying: "If your arrogance allows you to think you can keep the law and live a perfect life apart from God, make sure you keep the whole law or you fail in all of it". Also under the Old Covenant, the penalty for being unable to abide by the law was death; both physical and spiritual. Spiritual death occurred at the time of each act of disobedience or violation of a specific part of the law. Physical death occurred through old age, which did not exist prior to Adam's disobedience, and would occur later in the person's life.

Under the Old Covenant Law, confession was made to God to obtain forgiveness of sins. This was accomplished through the priest. Under grace in the New Covenant, there is no requirement for confession of sins to God for the purpose of gaining forgiveness since all sins were completely forgiven at the Cross. The sole purpose of confession to God in the New Covenant, under grace, is so that we can be in "agreement" with Him as to what those sins are and to the specific reasons why we entered them. This is so we can examine what was going on in our lives at that time that would have led us to that action or thought so we would not engage in those sins again. Confession of our faults to gain forgiveness under grace is made between all men out of love (James 5:16); not to God. As we offend each other and through our love, compassion, and understanding, we can encourage a brother or sister's Christian walk by forgiving them without condemnation, thus helping them not to stumble again. We can do the same for non-Christians with the hope that God will use us as vehicles to show grace and love.

Through God's mercy, we are covered by grace, where Jesus has paid the required penalty for our sins on the Cross in the eyes of

God. Man's responsibility is to accept Christ as his Savior in full realization that, even with his best human efforts and works, he has no chance of ever keeping the law (of the Old Covenant) and being made perfect. Without accepting Christ as Savior and becoming born again, man's sin nature and the sins committed out of that sin nature, is not forgiven. Without redemption of this sin nature, we are unable to enter the presence of a Holy, pure and perfect God who is unable to be in the presence of that unjustified sin nature. Although (as Christians) we are under grace where our righteousness before God is established with our identity in Christ separate from good works and deeds, we still sometimes try to come to God through keeping the Old Covenant Law (or parts of it) which have a righteous and logical human appeal to us. This is sometimes referred to as "Galatianism". This is because of our pride, our need to control, and our attempts to establish our own system of justification and what is right before God, along with other carnal desires.

We want to be like God and control destiny and circumstances. Many people disagree with the principles of grace because if others are controlled by grace and the mercy of Christ, they themselves (as a pastor, elder, deacon or teacher) are unable to control others in a religious system or sect and impart guilt when people do wrong and sin. It is unfortunate that the primary role and identity in Christ of these legalistic "stewards of truth and righteous living" is that of insecure watchdogs where their relationship with God consists of punitive monitoring and enforcement. God will never violate a man or a woman's will. He gives us the right and dignity to choose eternal life, as established by his provision, or to choose a life apart from Him. The true love God has for us is evidenced by the free choice he empowers us with – to choose to live without Him if that is our desire.

The Old Covenant and Ten Commandment Law Pointing To The New Covenant and Grace

The Old Testament book of Leviticus (17:11) states that the life of the body is in the blood and that blood was given to man (and required by him) to use at the alter for the atonement of all sins. From God's perspective, and true for both the Old and New Covenants in the Bible, it is blood and only blood which can act as atonement or forgiveness for sins. It is understood this may not be very appealing to our own carnal nature or our sense of human logic based on world views, but this is Biblical. In the Old Testament, the blood used for this atonement was that of bulls and goats by the priest. In the New Covenant the blood sacrifice for forgiveness is that of Jesus.

The Ten Commandments and the Law foreshadowed the opportunity of perfection to come through Christ and His message of grace. As stated in Hebrews 10:9-10, God takes away the first Covenant (The Old Covenant based on the Law) so that He may establish the second Covenant (The New Covenant based on grace and love). We are justified through the offering of the body of Christ once for all if we accept this free gift. Bob George (People To People Ministries Dallas Texas), tells us that human history is not divided into (B.C.) Before Christ and (A.D.) Anno Domino. It is divided at the Cross; at the death of Christ. Jesus preached while he lived during the time of the Old Covenant however, he preached concerning the Good News of the New Covenant which would come, and could only come, after His death. At the time of His death, He would send the Holy Comforter (the Holy Spirit). The Holy Spirit could only come and permanently indwell in each believer if Christ died.

The New Covenant is established (and begins) by the blood of Christ at the time of His death and resurrection. Hebrews 9:16-22 tells us that where a will or testament exists, there must by necessity, be the death of the testator (the person who the will refers to). Hebrews 9 is referring to the death of Christ (being the testator) and is representative of the ending of the Old Covenant and the beginning of the New Covenant. Hebrews 9 reminds us that a will or testament is of force only after a person dies; otherwise, it is of no strength at all while the testator lives. Essentially, a will is not in effect until the death of the person whom the will refers to. Likewise, the Old Covenant (first testament) was not dedicated without blood. Hebrews 9 tells us that when Moses had spoken all critical points to all the people according to the law, he took the blood of calves and goats and sprinkled both the book and all the people saying: This is the blood of the testament and covenant which God has joined to you. He also sprinkled with blood both the tabernacle and all the vessels of the ministry. Moses also stated that all things are by the law purged with blood; and <u>without shedding of blood there is no remission</u>. From this, we understand there can never be any forgiveness of sin, or justification of a sin-nature, under the Christian way of life, unless there is the shedding of blood.

The book of Hebrews tells us that the annual days of atonement of sin (during the Old Covenant) never made anything perfect. The sacrifices of animals in the Old Covenant merely deferred our being judged for the sins we had committed to a future point in time (usually the following year) or until the next time we sinned. The sacrifices under the old system (during the Old Covenant) were repeated continuously, year after year by the priests, but they could never permanently save those who lived under their rules – and they never made anything perfect. If they could have, one offering by the priests would have been enough; the worshipers to God would have been made perfect once and for all, and their guilt would be gone.

However, the exact opposite happened since Biblically, it is not possible for the blood of animals (or any priest) to ever <u>take away</u> sins completely for all time. The blood of these animals was only capable of <u>temporarily</u> atoning for sins. Before the Law was given to Moses there was sin in the world but there was no punishment for it. After the Law was given to the people, they then had a standard to live by; a standard (or measuring stick) for which they could judge their actions; almost like a mirror that could reflect their actions which they never had before. Instead, there was then a monitoring or evaluation instrument in place to reflect the sin that showed man's sinfulness; sinfulness which was generated by the existence of the sin nature inside him.

Christ did not come to condemn or accuse us. The Mosaic Law did that because it provided a standard for which to compare our actions to; actions that we as humankind thought would earn us a way to Heaven. Further, it is our own actions which judge us when we are honest and objective enough to accurately compare them to God's expectations of our lives.

Christ, in John 16:7-9, states that it is important He leave this earth so that the Holy Spirit may appear, since this Spirit could not enter this world and indwell permanently in each of us until He was gone. In this way, it is possible for believer Christians to be indwelt with the Holy Spirit; not just visited occasionally by it – as was the case under the Old Covenant.

Purpose Of, And Limitations With, The Old Covenant And The Law It Was Based On

God found fault with man, not with His original Covenant (the Law and Ten Commandments). This fault with man was his inability to live a perfect life without sin based on his actions, works and own moral compass. For this reason, God needed to make a New Covenant with man. Mankind could not live by the law of the Old Covenant He had created (based on the request of humankind), so He needed to give them a different way. This would be a Covenant with expectations that would be more according to man's abilities; or more accurately, his inabilities. Galatians 2:21 states: I do not compromise the grace of God: for if righteousness was able to come by the law, then Christ is dead in vain and without purpose. Hebrews 8:6-10,12 states: But now He has obtained a more perfect and excellent ministry, and He is the mediator of a better Covenant (the New Covenant), which was established on better promises. For if that first Covenant (Old Covenant) had been faultless, then there should not have been a purpose for the second. For finding fault with them, he said, behold, the days come, when I will make a New Covenant...Not according to the Covenant that I made with their fathers (Old Covenant); because they were not able to keep that Covenant.

The Old Covenant law then, made nothing perfect and the deeds of trying to abide by the law were not able to justify any man; only point him to a new spiritual path that could. In John 5:45 (paraphrased), Jesus accuses the Sadducees of trusting in the Mosaic law as the way to heaven; in essence, for holding onto the Old Covenant and not believing in the New. Romans 3:20 tells us that by the deeds of the Old Covenant law, no person can be justified in his sight; for by the law is the knowledge of sin. In this verse, God is directing us towards His New Covenant which is based on love, mercy, grace and a higher personal calling and expectation guided by the Holy Spirit; not driven by fear, law and penalty.

Hebrews 7:18,19 states that: The Old Covenant law made nothing perfect, but the bringing in of a better hope did; by which we were able to draw closer to God. If perfection and spiritual completeness could be obtained by observing the Law of Moses, there would have been no reason for Christ to come and die for the sins of the world. Hebrews 7:11,12 states that: If perfection were by the Levitical priesthood, (for under it the people received the law), what further need was there that another priest should rise after the order of Melchisedec (after the order of another Old Covenant High priest based on keeping the Law)?

The issue of forgiveness was different under the Ten Commandment Law. All year long God kept a record of people's transgressions and the guilt that came with it under the Law. In the Old Covenant people lived in fear of God's punishment which was threatened for transgressions of the law. The Day of

Atonement was the annual time of fasting and prayer and a time to confess one's sins. It was the day each year when the perfect bull was sacrificed on behalf of the people and the nation of Israel. It was a time when the high priest, representing man and as a mediator to God, took sacrificial blood and went behind the veil in the Holy of Holies. Under the Old Covenant with man, God kept an accurate record of what sins we were guilty of in the previous year. In the New Covenant under grace, God does not keep record of these sins since, for the believer, they are forgiven at the Cross. The Bible tells us that God is love. In the 13th chapter of I Corinthians, love is outlined to us and is described as not involving keeping the record of someone else's sins. This is not only an example for how we should demonstrate our love towards others in the New Covenant but is also an example and model as to the true dynamics of God's love for us.

It could be asked then; was the law contrary to God's original promise and intention for man, especially since it is viewed as an imperfect system by so many? God's system (the Old Covenant) was not imperfect. It was the imperfection of man which led to the failure of this plan by God. Galatians 3: 21-23 states that: Is the law then against the promises of God? No, for if there had been a law given which could have given life, righteousness should have been by the law. But the Scripture has concluded all under sin that the promise by faith of Christ might be given to them that believe. But before faith came, we were kept under the law, shut up unto the faith which should afterwards be revealed. According to the Bible, the greatest sin is the sin of unbelief, and this sin yields eternal separation from God (spiritual death). Romans 5:13-21 state that sin is not imputed unless there is a law and that the Ten Commandments were given so that man could see the extent of his failures and inability to live a perfect life. Sin ruled over all men and brought them to death. Galatians 3:19 states that (paraphrased): What then is the purpose of the law? It was added because of transgressions, until the seed (Jesus) should come to whom the promise was made.

In the Old Covenant, the high priest was our mediator. In the New Covenant, Christ is our mediator between us and God. The New Covenant establishes standards which man, with all his shortcomings, can attain. Galatians 3:10,11 explains that no man is made righteous by observing the law: If you continue to try and make your justification based on keeping the Law, make sure you keep the entire Law and don't break any of its provisions. But that no man is justified by the law in the sight of God, it is evident: for, the just shall live by faith (paraphrased). It is important to note here that there is a big difference between just believing in something and putting full faith in it. Putting full faith in something means trusting it spiritually, emotionally, and in the depths of the heart. Believing in something can involve only the head knowledge of something or understanding it on an intellectual logical level, without full commitment from the self emotionally, spiritually, or physically.

In the Old Covenant, man was seen by God as not being responsible enough to act as ministers of that Covenant. Instead, a priest was necessary to be the minister. In the New Covenant, expectations are different. II Corinthians 3:6 states that we are not to follow the letter of the law but the spirit: We are made able ministers of the New Testament; not of the letter, but of the spirit; for the letter kills, but the spirit gives life. Under the New Covenant we are to have confidence that we can enter God's presence and that God lives in us through His Holy Spirit at the time of our salvation in Christ. Hebrews 10:19 tells us we are to have the boldness to enter the Holiest of Holies through the blood of Jesus. In his research, Bob George (People To People Ministries) points out that the word "faith" was only used 15 times in the Old Testament and then, only in relation to the relationship between a husband and wife, or in relation to the entire nation of Israel. The word "faith" was never used in the Old Testament in relation to one person's relationship with God. This should be clear to us, as participants in the New Covenant, that the Old Covenant was not designed for man to have a personal relationship with God through faith. Instead, that relationship was dependent on man's ability to observe and keep the Mosaic legalistic and mechanical Ten Commandment laws through good deeds, works and actions.

Romans 7:1-4 tells us that the law has dominion over a man as long as he lives. Romans continues by saying that a woman who is married is bound by the law to her husband until he dies. When he dies, she is free from the law of marriage to him. Similarly, we have become dead to the Old Covenant law through the body of Christ so that we may be married to another – to Him who raised us from the dead (Christ). Essentially, God's intention for us is to view ourselves as being dead to the Old Covenant law so we are free to enter a new union with God under the New Covenant where love and grace are our masters as given by the example of Christ.

Reflection & Study Questions For This Chapter:

- Were Adam and Eve given a completely free choice to eat or not eat from the Tree of Knowledge?
- How is this similar to the choices God gives each of us today?
- What are the key principles in the Old Covenant and Ten Commandment Law which point all people towards the New Covenant and Grace?
- What was the purpose of, and limitations of, the Old Covenant and Law it was based on?

Chapter 2

Foundations Of Biblical Salvation

God created us to have life and enjoy it, to praise and fellowship with Him, to use our gifts for His glory and to love others. Through our pride, arrogance, desire to control things, and other characteristics of the carnal self, we were never to believe we were equal to or greater than Him or that we had His knowledge or omnipotence. Yet the Biblical version of man's fall in the Garden of Eden by Adam eating from the forbidden Tree of Knowledge represented just such a belief and attitude. This fall caused all of humankind to be born with a sin-nature. Adam and Eve were not forbidden to eat of the Tree of Life in the Garden of Eden; however, only the Tree of Knowledge. The Tree of Life appears briefly in the beginning of the book of Genesis but does not re-appear until the Book of Revelation in the Bible.

This progression was all part of God's perfect plan to show humankind the extent to which we would develop logical methods (based on our own wisdom) to please God according to standards based on our own efforts, works and self-directed acts of good. 2000 years of mankind's efforts to keep and abide by the law proved futile where no one was able to keep and abide by it. Essentially, God (based on our desires and hearts) had given us a plan in the Old Covenant to show us we could not live by it.

Man was created as a three part being: body, soul and spirit. The body allows us to understand the world through our sensory experiences or through empirical knowledge. The soul (mind and intellect) gives man consciousness of self; the ability to be a unique person and have a personality. The spirit gives man the ability to communicate with God, understand His Will, and discern the things of the Holy Spirit. The soul of man represents his personality, consciousness of self and personal life. The work of the soul is said to act as a balance; to keep the body as the lowest and in subjection to the Spirit, which is the highest. The spirit of people is the part of us which can best communicate with and understand God and His purpose for us. God is a Spirit (John 4:24), and the spirit of man is the part which resembles God most. Ecclesiastes 12:7 tells us that, at death, the body goes to the dust and the spirit goes to God; for Him to judge. Romans 8:1,4 tell us that our likes and dislikes change when we give our spirit over to God, as clay is given to a potter to shape and form. According to the New Covenant, if we are saved, we are said to be dead to the desires of our body yet we have a living soul and spirit. If, through our own choice, we are not saved in this world, we have a living body, a living soul, but a dead spirit which will never share eternity with God.

Christ was sent by God to give us a more perfect sacrifice and method to eliminate the need for the annual Day of Atonement of the Old Covenant (Old Testament) and to eliminate the need to worry and constantly be concerned with our spiritual status (righteous standing) before God. This method is eternal salvation from our sin-nature through recognizing our need for a Savior and indeed, Christ as that Savior. In accepting Christ as our Savior, we are "born again" believers; believers who have a new spiritual birth and an entire new identity as seen by God being spiritually perfect and eternally forgiven. He is the one who saves us from the result of having a sin nature, which in having without God's forgiveness prevents us from entering His presence. Jesus came to take away the sins of the world, not merely to cover them up for a time. He was sent to us by God who was not willing that anyone in this world would perish and die without eternal salvation. To fully understand God's invitation to us in the New Covenant, as proclaimed in the New Testament, why we need to be saved, and how we can be saved into spiritual security; let's look at some scriptural passages.

Why we need to be saved:

Genesis 8:21	The imagination of man's heart is evil from the time we are very young.
Romans 3:23	Everyone in this world has sinned and comes short of God's amazing glory.
Ecclesiastes 7:20	There is not a just man on the earth that does good and never sins.
Genesis 6:5	God saw the wickedness of man was great on this earth and every imagination of the thoughts of his heart were evil.
Romans 3:10	There is no one who is righteous in this world without God; not one.
Romans 6:23	The payment of sin is death: but the gift of God is eternal life through Jesus Christ; Lord and Savior.

God's spiritual invitation to us:

Revelations 3:20	I stand at the door of your heart and knock and say: If any man hears my voice, and opens the door, I will come into him, and will be with him and him with me.
II Peter 3:9	It is not the Lord's intention or desire that any person should perish but instead, all should come to repentance and accept Jesus as savior.
John 3:3	The only way you can see the kingdom of God is to be born again.
II Corinthians 6:2	Do not wait since now is the acceptance time of salvation; now is the day of salvation.
John 6:37	Christ tells us that the Father gives us an assurance, that he who comes to me with a repentant humble heart I will in no way cast out.
Matthew 11:28	Come to me all you that labor and are heavy laden in your hearts and I will give you rest.

How we can be saved from the eternal effects of our sin nature:

Acts 16:31	If you believe on the Lord Jesus Christ as your savior, you shall be saved.
Acts 2:21	Whoever that will call on the name of the Lord will be saved.
Ephesians 2:8,9	It is by grace that you are saved through faith; and that not of yourselves: it is the gift of God. Not of works, that any man should boast or brag.
I Peter 2:24	Christ bore our sins in his own body on the tree so that we, being dead to our sins, could live into righteousness and it was by the stripes he received and through His death that you were healed.
John 3:16	God loved the world so much that he gave his only Son, that whoever would believe in him should not perish, but has everlasting life.
John 3:7	Do not marvel or be amazed that I said to you, you must be born again.
I John 5:13	Believe on the name of the Son of God; that you may know that you have eternal life, and that you may believe on the name of the Son of God.
Romans 6:4	Therefore, we are buried with him by baptism unto death: that like as Christ was raised up from the dead by the glory of the Father, even so we also should walk in the newness of life.
Romans 10:9-13	If you would confess with your mouth the Lord Jesus, and shall believe in your heart that God has raised him from the dead, you shall be saved. For with the heart man believes unto righteousness and with the mouth confession is made unto salvation. For whosoever shall call upon the name of the Lord will be saved.

Receiving Christ as Savior:

Acts 4:12	There is salvation in no other; for there is no other name under heaven given among men, whereby we must be saved.
John 14:6	Jesus said, I am the way, the truth, and the light; no man comes unto the Father but by me.
John 1:12	As many as received him, to them gave he power to become the sons of God, even to them that believe on his name.

The new birth involves being made a new creature by the power of the Holy Spirit. It is a new creation, a second birth, and after its occurrence in our lives, we are called "a new person" (Ephesians 4:24; Colossians 3:10). Regeneration, or becoming born-again, has no substitute and failing to become born-again means the individual is "lost" in (and to) this world. The Holiness of God requires us to become born-again, as is stated in Hebrews 12:14, through the Word of God (I Peter 1:23) and through the Spirit of God (John 3:5-8). The evidence of this regeneration is an increase in righteous living from our works (James), a greater awareness and sense of what is right and wrong according to God's perspective, a greater love of our neighbors and others, and living not according to the world's standards but instead, living more by God's standards under grace and the higher expectations established by God under the New Covenant.

Salvation does not occur automatically through baptism of water; entering a confession booth; joining a church; walking a church aisle to dedicate our lives to God in the eyes of others; confirmation of a faith never originally accepted and realized; performance of good works; living by man's invented spiritually legalistic standards; becoming one or 'self-actualized' with our positive inner being or self through a process of enlightenment; or by accomplishing great things according to our own intuition, standard or invention of what we intellectually or emotionally believe is the way to Heaven. Salvation occurs for us (individually) when we not only accept that we have a spiritual sin-nature and because of this, that we need a Savior, but also accept that God sent Christ to die for our sins (the source of that sin-nature) – so that our sin nature may be forgiven and made righteous through His death. If we accept this sacrifice from God as a free gift, one that we do not earn or work to obtain or deserve through our own merits, and that this forgiveness results in us having a new spiritual identity in the finished work of Christ; we have become born again spiritually. This new spiritual identity means we are pure in the sight of God, worthy to enter His presence into Heaven, because the one whom we believe on (Christ) is perfect, and for no other reason – not even the great works and deeds we are sometimes able to accomplish. The Bible says that, following this act of commitment to God's word resulting in salvation, and as an outward sign of an inward change, we are to be baptized according to Acts 9:18, 8:36-38, and 16:33.

Through His Holy Spirit, we are guided and directed in our life's walk to do God's will, through trials and tribulations as well as by experiencing tremendous joy, peace, security, acceptance, and happiness for this life. As born-again Christians (after such time as we have accepted Christ as our Savior), we can spiritually discern many things which otherwise could not be understood or comprehended by a non-believer or unsaved individual (I Corinthians 2:14, Proverbs 1:23, 21:2, and Psalms 119:18). The primary reason for this is that the working of God's Holy Spirit is then in us and with His guidance and direction, and through the humility we have as a new creature, we are more aware of good and evil, Godliness and un-Godliness, and the difference between being perfect and being forgiven.

After such time as an individual has been saved, there is a constant daily renewal in his/her life (II Corinthians 4:16, Psalms 51:10, Isaiah 40:31). This is not to say that the individual constantly is being spiritually reborn or born again; again and again. There are many misconceptions of this in our churches of today which incorrectly focuses the believer too much on how he/she "feels" instead of the steadfast knowledge and complete certainty of being 100% confident we have become born again, and that this identity lasts forever, unchanged. This is also not to say that the person is progressively more and more "justified" in the eyes of God. It is saying however, that God is showing us new awareness's, discoveries, and truths every day and giving us an opportunity to renew our original love for Him because of His love for us. It is a growing and a day-by-day increase of an already existing established faith, not a continuous beginning of a new commitment and faith (relating to our spiritual salvation). It is a process of us understanding more and more each day as to what God already knows about us in His infinite wisdom; but for which we do not understand about ourselves.

In the Old Testament and Old Covenant, the imagined possibility of perfection was accomplished through our own actions and by observance of the Law. Additionally, our gifts to God were required to be perfect as well (Genesis 17:1, Deut. 18:13, Job 1:1, Psalms 101:2,6 & Leviticus 22:21). Hebrews 7:11,19, 9:9 and 10:1 tells us that this Old Covenant Law made nothing perfect, however. In the New Covenant with man, God tells us that spiritual righteousness and purity comes at the time the individual becomes "born-again" (Luke 6:40, John 17:23, I Corinthians 2:6, Galatians 3:3, Colossians 1:28, Hebrew 10:14, and Hebrews 12:23). The perfection (sanctification) of the individual's soul takes place throughout the life of the person in this world through trials and tribulations as well as through the experience of blessings from God. The perfection of the soul involves a lifetime of character building through growing in Grace and the on-going process of sanctification in the New Covenant as guided by the Holy Spirit (Matthew 5:48, 19:21, II Corinthians 12:9, 13:11, Ephesians 4:12,13, Philippians 3:12, Colossians 4:12, II Timothy 3:17, Hebrews 2:10, 6:1, 13:21, James 1:4, 2:22, 3:2, I Peter 5:10, and I John 2:5, 4:12-17).

The Bible tells us that there is but one God; eternal, infinite, perfect, and unchangeable. He exists and reveals himself in three persons – Father, Son, and Holy Spirit (Deuteronomy 6:4, Psalm 90:2, Genesis 17:1, Isaiah 40:23, 57:15, Malachi 3:6, Genesis 1:2, Hebrews 1:8, 13:8, Matthew 28:19). It is clearly God's Will for each individual to have a personal relationship with Him through the example and mediation of Jesus Christ. After becoming born again, and through this submission of God's Will within our lives, we are then able to experience the fullest potential of what our lives can be through realizing all of the blessings God had planned for us; blessings of great joy and happiness but also blessings through our experience of trials and tribulations; both yielding tremendous growth, peace and spiritual awareness for us.

Reflection & Study Questions For This Chapter:

- Why do you think God created us?
- Why do we need to be saved spiritually?
- What is God's invitation to us for salvation?
- How do we become saved?
- Once we are saved, what does our new spiritual identify mean in God's eyes? In your eyes? In the eyes of others?

Chapter 3

The Permanence Of Salvation

Knowing that Christian salvation is not temporary but permanent, born-again believers can rest and be confident in the completeness of Christ's death on the Cross for them and therefore, can be fully committed in living in the grace, security, and unconditional love from God. With this permanent salvation, Christians can be concerned about engaging themselves completely in the full responsibility to live their lives unencumbered or uninhibited to glorify God with their unconditional love towards others.

However, if salvation is temporary and permanent only until a person commits a sin which places him/her "over the line" with God, the Christian has to then have tremendous concerns over where the line is in losing that salvation, how to gain it back once it is lost, and what happens if he/she dies in a state of sin having lost that salvation, while in the midst of trying to earn it back. This involves a tremendous amount of emotional, physical, and spiritual energy that is dedicated to all these nerve provoking questions; energy which could otherwise be used in presence showing full unconditional love towards others and in more fully comprehending God's perfect will and path based on the peace, security, confidence and unconditional positive regard from God. When Satan keeps our hearts and minds occupied with constantly wondering about the permanence of our salvation and our standing with God, he is succeeding in sidetracking our focus, complete attention, and full commitment to use our gifts to serve God.

The review of the following Scriptures is intended to show that Christian salvation is permanent and, knowing this, to put in perspective versus that have been improperly used to support the incorrect viewpoint that Christian salvation is temporary. This review intentionally does not include any verses from the Old Testament because the issue of salvation being permanent or temporary cannot be objectively examined under the standard of the Old Covenant law on which the Old Testament rests. This viewpoint is clearly reflected in Romans 7 and 8 as well as numerous chapters in Hebrews. Additionally, Paul scolds the brethren in Galatians 3 and demonstrates full testimony to this point where he states: You foolish Galatians, you did not obtain or secure your salvation by your works and deeds or anything that you have merited so what makes you think you can keep your salvation based on your works. Additionally, multiple places in the Bible tell us that we are no longer under the Old Covenant law and that it was only there to bring us to the reality of needing Christ as our Savior under the New Covenant.

The review of each specific verse in this chapter consists of three parts: A.) A verse which has been commonly used to justify the position of salvation being temporary, B.) An explanation as to why advocates of temporary salvation believe this verse proves or adds credibility to their viewpoint, and C.) The author's statement (apologetics) which contradicts the explanation provided and discounts the rationale under which it is being used to support the temporary salvation position.

Luke 9:62

"And Jesus said to him, no man, having put his hand to the plough, and looking back, is fit for the kingdom of God."

Statement of temporary salvation: "Putting his hand to the plough" refers to the individual making a commitment to Christ and becoming a saved and born again Christian. If the individual then looks back or sins according to his old ways and sin nature, he is not fit for the kingdom of God and therefore loses his salvation.

Statement of permanent salvation: It is incorrect to say that the phrase "having put his hand to the plough" necessarily refers to an individual who has already put his hand (and heart) towards salvation, and is therefore saved. Going back several verses in Luke 9:55 and 56, Christ is speaking to people who are not in fact saved, and they do not know the spirit of their true human nature, which is corrupt. The phrase "putting your hands to the plough" refers to an individual who is ready to make a commitment to Christ, but hasn't done that as of yet. It is saying that if we know (intellectually) that Christ's love can save us, and have begun the mental process of committing, but we have no intention as of yet of following through and completely surrendering ourselves to Him and believing on Him as our Savior - then we are not fit for the kingdom of God. Essentially, the only commitment God wants from us at the time we surrender to Him and accept Christ as our Savior is that of a total and full commitment. God does not want, and will not accept, anything less. As we see Him as a perfect and Holy God, we would expect nothing less from Him. Additionally, looking at the next chapter of Luke (10:21), it is evident that God sometimes hides the truth to the prudent and wise and gives it instead to babes, the innocent, the humble, and the meek. Not only does God require a full commitment from us, but He will sometimes allow our own pride, stubbornness, and human wisdom to interfere with His will for us. This is not His doing; it is our own consequences for repeatedly rejecting Him over and over again. It is a reflection of the free choice he gives to us.

Hebrews 6:4-6

"For it is impossible for those who were once enlightened and have tasted of the heavenly gift and were made partakers of the Holy Ghost and have tasted the good Word of God and the powers of the world to come; if they shall fall away, to renew them again to repentance; seeing they crucify to themselves the Son of God afresh, and put him to an open shame."

Statement of temporary salvation: It is impossible for those who were once born again to be renewed unto repentance, if they ever fall away by sinning, and reject God's great love for us in the person of Jesus Christ.

Statement of permanent salvation: The word "partakers", in Hebrews 3:12-14, was shown to be those who have not yet fully made a commitment to Christ. They were in route and in the process but had not fully believed. Partakers and believers are two different things. Partaker is one who passively shares with. A believer is one who fully believes.

It should never be automatically assumed that because a Christian believer has sinned and fallen, that he necessarily is unable to be restored through a confession (agreement) with God. In times of anger and frustration, we have all doubted the existence or true love of God (or sinned in other ways) while we remained Christians. As Christians, we have all sinned and will continue to sin. The entire life of a Christian is spent in a process of renewal, sinning and learning from those sins through confession (agreement). We call this growing in grace and being sanctified through trials and tribulations which build our character and prepare us for an eternity with God. As we get more and more mature in our Christian walk, we sin less and less, but we still sin, and we still have periods in our lives where we doubt God and His will and question His ways. Hebrews 6:4-6 is not written concerning born again believers slipping into sin, falling away, and not being able to be restored. Instead, these verses were written to unbelievers who have heard the entire Gospel message and understood it completely with their minds and intellect – but yet had not made a commitment with their heart. <u>If they reject this message after such time as it has been explained to them, and that they have fully understood it with their mind and intellect, there is nothing more that can be done to help them understand it any more completely. It can't be explained to them by someone standing on their head, by speaking another language, or by yelling and being more emotional.</u> They already understand it, they are just not willing to commit with their heart to it. Therefore, God leaves them to their own folly and unbelief.

This is the essence of God's love for us in terms of allowing us a free choice to believe or disbelieve, even after such time as we have completely heard and understand, but do not follow through with a total heart commitment. In these situations, God says that there can be nothing left to do for the individual except to entitle him to his own reality, and leave him in his state of unbelief – which, sadly, is what he wanted anyway. John 5:24 tells us that he who believes on the name of Christ has everlasting life and shall never come under condemnation. The fact is that there are many people in this world, and people who lived in Biblical times, who professed, as well as were seen, to be believers, yet who were in fact not believers at all. I Corinthians 15:2 supports this and states that we should keep in memory that which we have heard relating to the Gospel message, unless we have believed in vain (and never actually made a true and full commitment).

Hebrews 10:25-29

"Not forsaking the assembling of ourselves together, as the manner of some is; but exhorting one another: and so much the more, as you see the day approaching. For if we sin willfully after that we have received the knowledge of the truth, there remains no more sacrifice for sins."

See temporary and permanent salvation statement for Hebrews 6:4-6 (above) for responses to this verse.

II Corinthians 13:5

"Examine yourselves, whether you be in the faith; prove your own selves. Know you not your own selves, how that Jesus Christ is in you, except you be reprobates?"

Statement of temporary salvation: It is assumed that those who Paul is talking to are saved and have been born again. The true Christians who are the object of Paul's focus are supposed to examine themselves daily to make sure they have not lost their faith through sin and therefore their salvation. If they find they have lost their salvation because of some sin they have committed, they are therefore referred to as reprobates. (A reprobate is one who has been rejected and has reversed his/her beliefs because of moral depravity, wickedness, or an action which requires God's condemnation).

Statement of permanent salvation: If we examine several verses which precede II Corinthians 13:5, we can see why this cannot be used to justify or help explain the temporary salvation theory. II Corinthians 13:3 tells us that the people Paul is talking to are not, in fact, saved. Therefore, how could anyone be a true reprobate as defined by the temporary salvation camp (a person who has reversed his spiritual beliefs to be against God and lost their salvation) if they never knew Him or believed in Him to begin with? Verse 3 tells us these individuals are still seeking proof of Christ's divinity, which would certainly not qualify them for those who are saved based on a total and complete commitment of believing on the name of Christ as their Lord and personal Savior. II Corinthians 13:5, contrary to the temporary salvation interpretation, tells the non-believers at Corinth to examine themselves to make sure that they have given their hearts to Christ, which, by the warnings stated by Paul, does not seem has occurred. As non-believers, Paul identifies them as reprobates, because they have repeatedly heard the Gospel message with their mind and intellect, and have begun to trust, but have not believed totally with their hearts onto Christ as their Savior, and on His resurrection to give them life.

John 8:31

"Then Jesus said to those Jews who believed on him, if you abide in my Word, you are My disciples indeed;"

Statement of temporary salvation: If someone is a disciple of Christ, he will continue in the Word of God and never sin. If the person does not continue in His Word and keep from sinning (or committing too many sins), then he is not a disciple of Christ and therefore loses his salvation.

Statement of permanent salvation: To gain a complete understanding of how God would have us interpret this verse, let's look at John 8:37. In that verse, Christ is speaking to a group of individuals where His Word has no place in their heart, and therefore were never saved to begin with. They believed on Him with their mind and intellect and understood His Words in that context, but have not made a full commitment with their heart. Stating that John 8:31 supports the concept of temporary salvation is incorrect and is taking it out of context. Additionally, John 8:32 tells us that if we understand the full truth of God's message of a New Covenant with mankind and have accepted Christ as our Savior (which diminishes our sin-nature), we have then been set free. Believing that, if we sin again (which all Christians do every day) we can lose this precious salvation that God has given us, does not sound much like complete and total spiritual freedom – freedom to love others without fear of rejection and failure as well as freedom to focus on God's will for us (instead of constantly wondering when our salvation will be lost – and thinking about when it will return if we lose it.) I Corinthians 15:2 states that - "By which ye are also saved, if ye keep in memory what I preached unto you, unless ye have believed in vain." This is an additional verse which emphasizes the real possibility that sometimes, when we see people living what we perceive to be a "carnal Christian" life, it may just be that they were never saved to begin with.

Hebrews 2:1

"Therefore, we ought to give the more earnest heed to the things which we have heard, lest at any time we should let them slip."

Statement of temporary salvation: If we aren't careful about the things we have heard within the Gospel message and making sure that we continue to perform good works and deeds and not sin, then our salvation will slip and we will lose it.

Statement of permanent salvation: Hebrews 2:1 is not speaking to persons who are already saved. To put Hebrews 2:1 into proper perspective, we can look at some surrounding verses since it is oftentimes dangerous to look at a single verse and build a doctrine from it. For example, Hebrews 2:3 tells us that if we neglect to commit in accepting this free gift God has given us in the Lord Jesus Christ, after hearing His clear message, we will be judged harshly by Him. Hebrews 2:3 is speaking about an individual who has not been saved yet and this is also true of Hebrews 2:1. We can know this by examining its preceding verse Hebrews 1:14 which states that the angels are spirit messengers sent to minister to those who will one day, in the future, receive salvation.

If we look at this verse and assume (incorrectly) that it is referring to a saved person, we see that the phrase "let them slip" in Hebrews 2:1 is translated in the original Greek to mean "run out as leaking vessels". Let them slip has a connotation of a specific action and a certain point in time whereas, running out as leaking vessels has more of a meaning which relates to a gradual and slow process or progressive development. If losing one's salvation is then a slow and gradual process, as would be stated by the temporary salvation camp, how would one know at what point they have lost that salvation? Would one person lose it at one point because he/she had more abilities than someone else and therefore God has a higher expectation of, but then someone who doesn't have as many talents and abilities would lose it at a later point? Would the different points of different people losing their salvation be determined by a group of 'fair minded' elders or would it be determined by each individual and their own sense of honesty and forthrightness to humbly provide daily accounts of their travels, in and out of salvation, to members of their church – or to themselves. Running out as leaking vessels is a good summary of what each Christian goes through each day and each hour of their lives in terms of their perfect spiritual walk with God; leaking out a little and then, through the grace of God and our indwelling Holy Spirit, being filled back up. It is a different way of saying what Paul is saying in Romans where he discusses his own personal battle with the sin nature (old man) inside him. It could easily refer to sins which we all commit and think of, therefore rendering us guilty of, whether we act on those lusts and motives or not.

Hebrews 3:12-14

"Take heed brethren, lest there be in any of you an evil heart of unbelief, in departing from the living God. But exhort one another daily, while it is called today; lest any of you be hardened through the deceitfulness of sin. For we are made partakers of Christ, if we hold the beginning of our confidence steadfast unto the end;"

Statement of temporary salvation: All brothers in Christ, who begin to not believe, sin and fall away from the Gospel message and God should take heed. We are in Christ and keep our salvation only as long as we hold those things true to the end which we have heard and know to be true.

Statement of permanent salvation: Hebrews 3:12-14 is not speaking about brothers in Christ, even though the term brethren is used. Brethren is an endearing term that was used to address all the congregation in Biblical times, even though the speaker at that time knew that there would be many among the congregation who were not brothers, or believers (just like what happens in our services today). This verse is speaking about those who have heard the Gospel message and are beginning to fully trust in it but whom have not yet made a complete and total commitment to Christ. It gives warning that, as potential believers who may one day be brand new born again Christians, those individuals must be very careful not to be swayed away from the Word by the deceitfulness of sin. They will share in Christ's heavenly glory only if they keep searching for the truth and eventually make a commitment to Christ. The fact that the word "brethren" is used to include those who are unsaved is also represented in Hebrews 3:15 and 16, but especially in Hebrews 3:19.

James 1:12

"Blessed is the man who endures temptation; for when he has been approved, he will receive the crown of life which the Lord has promised to those who love Him."

Statement of temporary salvation: If you don't give into temptation and keep from sinning (to the point where you may lose your salvation), you will receive the crown of life. It is inferred here that this crown refers to a place in Heaven as a born-again believer is entitled to.

Statement of permanent salvation: The book of James is written to Jewish believers. Jewish believers were still very much pre-occupied with a works-based doctrine. We are warned about this works based doctrine in many passages in Scripture, especially in the book of Galatians. This act of returning to maintaining your salvation by works after such time you are saved is often referred to as "Galatianism" and it is condemned by Paul. The Bible tells us that there are 5 crowns available to the Christian. These are 5 rewards for the Christian following God's perfect will for him/her while on this earth. Salvation is not a reward, it is a gift. Therefore, the word crown in this passage cannot be referring to salvation.

Colossians 1:21-23

"And you, who once were alienated and enemies in your mind by wicked works, yet now He has reconciled in the body of His flesh through death, to present you holy, and blameless, and above reproach in His sight—if indeed you continue in the faith, grounded and steadfast, and are not moved away from the hope of the gospel which you heard, which was preached to every creature under heaven, of which I, Paul, became a minister."

Statement of temporary salvation: You have been reconciled by God and if you continue in your faith and good works and do not sin, you will keep your salvation; but you need to be steadfast and grounded.

Statement of permanent salvation: Epaphras had come to Rome and told Paul there were false teachers in Colossae who were telling the people that the Christian faith was incomplete, and they should worship angels and follow certain rules and ceremonies. Paul wrote to the Colossians to oppose these false teachers and to remind them that Jesus' death was all they needed to be saved from their sins and that through Him, they were free from man-made rules. Colossians 1:23 is telling the Colossians to continue in their faith. This means that the Colossians should continue to believe and have faith in the one true Gospel that Christ did it all (and that it is finished) and not buy in to any false teachings.

As a Christian, we prove we are a child of God by citing God's word and His promise we are assured of having eternal salvation, that Christ did it all and that we need to do nothing else other than believe on His name to be saved. Eternal does not mean until the next time we sin; eternal means eternal. In this verse in Colossians, the word "if" is not a conditional statement but instead means "in as much as". Colossians 1:22, 23 says "You have been reconciled by God through Christ's death, to present yourself holy and blameless and above reproach in His sight – 'inasmuch' as you continue in the faith, grounded and steadfast and are not moved away from the hope of the gospel which you heard.

Continuing in the faith in this verse means continuing to believe and trust in the one true gospel that salvation comes from believing on the death of Christ – plus nothing else. This is the exact opposite of what these false teachers were advocating. To this end, we will remain grounded in the true Gospel as long as we keep this in mind. This verse does not refer to our salvation being predicated or contingent on us continuing to always do good works and not sin. If that were the case, each Christian would lose their salvation seven times each day. These versus also reference the importance of keeping this faith in mind as we carry out our Christian walk. They say that, before you were saved, you were dominated by wicked works yet now, as a saved Christian you have been reconciled in the eyes of God and indwelt with the Holy Spirit to guide you into living a life which is governed by the Spirit, a life of good works dedicated to loving others so that you are above reproach in His sight – if you continue (as your faith guides you) to stay focused on His will.

Additionally, I John 5:9-14 tells us that "He who believes in the Son of God has the witness in himself; he who does not believe God has made Him a liar, because he has not believed the testimony that God has given of His Son. And this is the testimony: that God has given us eternal life, and this life is in His Son. He who has the Son has life; he who does not have the Son of God does not have life. These things I have written to you who believe in the name of the Son of God, that you may know that you have eternal life, and that you may continue to believe in the name of the Son of God." The word continue here is similar to that used in Colossians 1 referring to the importance of each Christian continuing to believe in our completeness in Christ.

Matthew 13:4-6 (Refers also to Luke 8:13)

"And when he sowed, some seeds fell by the way side, and the fowls came and devoured them up: Some fell upon stony places, where they had not much earth: and forthwith they sprung up, because they had no deepness of earth: And when the sun was up, they were scorched; and because they had no root, and they withered away."

Statement of temporary salvation: "Fell by the way side" and "they withered away" refers to salvation falling or withering away in someone's life, after they have committed sin or "stepped outside" of God's will.

Statement of permanent salvation: These verses refer to Christ preaching in a parable at the sea side concerning those who will hear the Gospel message and respond to it. As is seen in Matthew 13:19, where Jesus explains His parable, "fell by the way side" refers to those who have heard the word of God but who do not yet understand it, and while they are trying to understand it, Satan enters and takes the Word away from them. Matthew 13:20, 21 states that "withering away refers to those who believe but who do not make a full commitment with their heart because the Word never took root, but only stayed with them for awhile, long enough for them to possibly comprehend certain parts of Christ's message, but not entirely." Therefore, these individuals would never be able to lose their salvation because they never had it to begin with.

II Peter 2:15,20

"Which have forsaken the right way, and are gone astray, following the way of Balaam the son of Bosor, who loved the wages of unrighteousness; For if after they have escaped the pollution of the world through the knowledge of the Lord and Savior Jesus Christ, they are again entangled therein, and overcome, the latter end is worse with them than the beginning."

Statement of temporary salvation: Those who have gone astray have strayed from their salvation, and therefore lost it. Also, if they have become saved and have become entangled in life's sins, it is worse for him than if he had never been born-again at all.

Statement of permanent salvation: These verses are not speaking to those who are saved or who have become born-again. They are addressed to those who are not saved. The intent of these verses is to convey to those who have not, or will not, believe that if they have heard the Gospel message and understood it – and have rejected it – that they will have little hope to be saved because nothing else will convince them. They will never receive another opportunity to hear the message for the first time again without rejecting it. Scripture clearly tells us however, that non-believers will be held responsible at the judgment day for what they have heard concerning the Gospel and therefore will have no excuse (John 16:9, II Peter 2:9,12,14, II Peter 2:21 and 3:5).

Matthew 24:13

"But he that shall endure unto the end, the same shall be saved."

Statement of temporary salvation: The belief here is that, if an individual, through good works, good deeds, and observing laws set up by God (and not engaging in sin), endures to the end with good behavior, then he shall keep his salvation.

Statement of permanent salvation: Chapter 24 of Matthew refers to what will happen upon the return of Christ to this earth, concerning His second coming. It tells us that leading up to the time when Christ will return to earth, many will be deceived by Satan who will bring iniquity, which will lead to many people's faith in God growing cold. However, verse 11 addresses verse 13 and tells us those false prophets will deceive many just before Christ's second coming. Looking at the analysis directly above relating to Matthew 13, and the discussion of those who "fell by the way side" and those who "withered away", there is a direct parallel to Matthew 24:13. Those enduring to the end, and therefore being saved, refers to those who, hear the Gospel message and do not understand it, but who keep searching and are trying to open up their hearts, and endure to the end without allowing themselves to be deceived by Satan - such that the little understanding they do have does not wither away or fall by the way side. Matthew 24:13 does not refer to someone who already has his/her salvation; it refers to someone who is still searching, and who (hopefully) having completed this search in the future, will accept Christ as their Savior.

Matthew 25:1-13

"Then shall the kingdom of heaven be likened unto ten virgins, which took their lamps, and went forth to meet the bridegroom. And five of them were wise, and five were foolish. They that were foolish took their lamps, and took no oil with them: But the wise took oil in their vessels with their lamps. While the bridegroom tarried, they all slumbered and slept. And at midnight there was a cry made, Behold, the bridegroom cometh; go ye out to meet him. Then all those virgins arose, and trimmed their lamps. And the foolish said unto the wise, Give us of your oil; for our lamps are gone out. But the wise answered, saying, Not so; lest there be not enough for us and you: but go ye rather to them that sell, and buy for yourselves. And while they went to buy, the bridegroom came; and they that were ready went in with him to the marriage: and the door was shut. Afterward came also the other virgins, saying, Lord, Lord, open to us. But he answered and said, Verily I say unto you, I know you not. Watch therefore, for ye know neither the day nor the hour wherein the Son of man cometh."

Statement of temporary salvation: Because they had brought no extra oil with them, the five virgins who ran out of oil are compared with an individual who has been saved but who, because of sins in his/her life and having Crossed over the line into performing too many acts of sin, "runs out of" blessings from God and therefore, loses his/her salvation. In this parable, the idea is that the lamp is likened to our salvation and our good works and deeds are likened to the oil. In verses 11 and 12, the five virgins who ran out of oil, and went to purchase more, then tried to enter into the bridegroom's estate and are told by him that he knows them not, and are then told that it is too late. The implication is that, because an individual's works aren't good enough (or if we wait too long to show them to others,) it will then be too late, and our Lord will reject us.

Statement of permanent salvation: The oil in the lamps of the five virgins (who did not buy enough) is analogous and refers to mankind approaching God according to His plan not their own; through believing on the death, burial, and resurrection of His Son Jesus Christ. Many approach God in their own way, setting up their own rules and standards to live by and incorrectly refer to themselves as inheritors of God's heavenly kingdom, without ever having received Christ as their personal Lord and Savior. God clearly tells us in His Word (relating to un-believers), that He will not always keep the door open for us over and over again. There will come a time where our hearts are hardened and we are no longer receptive to any part of His message, analogous to our own lamp burning out. As free moral agents, we have a choice as to whether or not we will accept salvation, but we do not have a choice as to how that must occur. God also tells us that no one knows the year, day or hour when Christ will return to set up His judgment seat. Therefore, we must be prepared by having already given our life over to Christ and be saved, not through our good deeds and works, but by accepting His death for the forgiveness of our sins thus providing us with a new nature.

Jude 24

"Now unto them that is able to keep from falling, and to present you faultless before the presence of His glory with exceeding joy."

Statement of temporary salvation: "Keep from falling and present you faultless" refers to maintaining yourself as a Christian being without fault and never falling otherwise you may lose your salvation before God.

Statement of permanent salvation: God's perfect goal for us is to present ourselves faultless before Him at our judgment day. We were not able to do this without the shed blood of Christ as non-believers and we certainly aren't able to do it as Christians. To say that if a Christian sins and falls (and becomes a person with fault) necessarily means that he/she will lose their salvation must mean that every Christian loses his/her salvation at least once every day for their entire life. It is almost impossible for a Christian (even with the Holy Spirit working through him/her) to lead a faultless life. Such a statement is not only arrogant but ignorant of God's true message under the New Covenant. We can try to live a faultless life but if Paul couldn't do it, how can we think we can. Our salvation transforms us and old things pass away in our lives that are inconsistent with God's Word. We become spiritually perfect at the time of our salvation not because of what we have done or will do (or will continue to do) but because of the shed blood of Christ and Him imputing His righteousness on us – and because of what He has done. It is because of this blood, and only because of this blood (and our acceptance of the free gift found in His sacrifice) that we truly are spiritually perfect. The rest of our lives as Christians, after the time of our salvation, is a process of God growing our personality and character in the direction of perfection; a perfection that will never be realized until the time of our death. This occurs by us making clear choices to get out of the way of the workings of the Holy Spirit in our lives so that we do not operate according to our own personal and carnal agendas but instead, according to His perfect Will for us.

I Timothy 4:16

"Take heed to yourself and to the doctrine. Continue in them, for in doing this you will save both yourself and those who hear you."

Statement of temporary salvation: If you continue in God's doctrine and not sin (too much), you will save yourself and many others.

Statement of permanent salvation: Paul is telling Timothy (as a young pastor) to keep using his gift of teaching, to not allow his testimony to be shipwrecked; to save himself in adhering to the true Gospel that he accepted. He is encouraging Timothy to stay true to the doctrine he was taught and had accepted as a Christian, and to persevere. God has a perfect plan for Timothy and Paul wants him to realize and be a recipient to that perfect plan and the spiritual blessings that will come from that. Paul also knows that Timothy has a gift to lead others to Christ and to encourage their walk if Timothy continues to preach the one true doctrine (Gospel). Paul is saying: "If you keep on teaching the way God has inspired you to do, God's perfect will for your walk (his complete expectation unencumbered by the world) will be saved and the integrity of it will not be damaged and, in the process, others will commit to Christ because of you, your teaching and your example.

Philippians 2:12

"…work out your salvation with fear and trembling".

Statement of temporary salvation: It is important for those who, after being saved, perform works and deeds which maintain their salvation and provide the blessings from God to keep that salvation.

Statement of permanent salvation: Philippians 1:6 precedes and introduces Philippians 2:12 and therefore, to fully understand the context of 2:12 it is important to examine this verse. This verse contradicts the temporary salvation interpretation and states that we must be confident, as born-again believers, that God, who has performed a good work in us (as believers) will continue that work until Christ's return to earth in the Second Coming. Philippians 2:13 states that God works in us to His will and to do of His good pleasure which further contradicts the temporary salvation interpretation. The will of God referred to here (and in Philippians

1:9, 29, 2:2-7 and 14-17) involves the Christian's love abounding in knowledge in His will and through the interaction with others and that the process of living out our salvation involves being likeminded, having the same love, and not doing anything through strife but instead in humility and to build up others more than oneself. These verses also state that we are to be likeminded with Christ and fulfill our obligation as Christians by being the complete servant of others. To some, this verse also implies that through our behavior, we should earn our continued salvation with fear in our hearts. God is not a God of fear, and our salvation is not a salvation out of fear.

John 15:1-8,14

"I AM the true vine, and my Father is the husband. Every branch in me that does not bear fruit he takes it away: and every branch that bears fruit, he purges it, that it may bring forth more fruit. Now you are clean through the word which I have spoken unto you. Abide in me, and I in you. As the branch cannot bear fruit of itself, except it abide in the vine; no more can you, except you abide in me. I am the vine, ye are the branches: He that abides in me, and I in him, the same brings forth much fruit: for without me ye can do nothing. If a man abide not in me, he is cast forth as a branch, and is withered; and men gather them, and cast them into the fire, and they are burned. If you abide in me, and my words abide in you, you shall ask what you will, and it shall be done unto you. Herein is my Father glorified, that you bear much fruit; so shall you be my disciples…You are my friends, if you do whatsoever I command you."

Statement of temporary salvation: If we are a branch (born-again believer) who is living on the vine (Christ) and we are not bearing fruit – we will be taken away. Along these lines, the only way we can be "in fellowship" with Christ is if we keep His commandments.

Statement of permanent salvation: Under the New Covenant, Christ commands us to love one another as we would love ourselves and what we do to the least of His we do to Him. This "agape" love that Christ speaks of in the New Testament includes the concept of unconditional love that we are to give to others without expectation that they would give back to us. This is the same unconditional love that God extends to us if we are under the redemptive grace of Christ's death, burial, and resurrection. Even if we are truly born-again Christians, we will continue to fail at following the commandment that Christ gave to us of loving our neighbor as ourselves. Certainly, as Christians, we will have a much better chance of coming closer to Christ's expectation of us in terms of loving others, but we will still fall short. The Holy Spirit will guide us and direct us, but we will still fail in terms of not being able to be completely perfect by our actions and works. Fortunately, we have already been made spiritually pure at the time we accepted Christ as our Savior. So, to say that we are Christ's friend only if we do whatever he commands us (by loving our neighbor perfectly) is not accurate.

"The branches that are not in Him and are not bearing fruit therefore being taken away", refers to a person who is not yet accepted Christ and therefore cannot be used according to God's purpose and perfect Will as a human being. For discussion sake, if we assume that this verse does refer to a saved Christian, we can realize that it is sometimes the case where a born again Christian can reach a point in his/her life where they stagnate, stop growing in the Lord, and become spiritually useless according to the gifts and talents they were given by God to demonstrate Christ-like love to others. Satan is able to deceive people and render their Christian walk ineffective, leading them into continued sin. Their salvation is not lost, however. In those situations, they become like any other Christian who falls into sin temporarily or is living a life contrary to God's expectation of them, <u>differing only in degrees of infraction</u>. We have been given an example by God how to love others (as demonstrated by Jesus), and it is our challenge to live as close to that expectation as is possible, knowing full well that it is virtually impossible to live perfect according to our actions, deeds, and just as importantly, our motives and thoughts (as Paul clearly outlines in Romans 7). It is like a father telling a son that he is not his son anymore if he does something drastic that the father severely disapproves of. No matter what, the son does not lose his position as being his son. The father may kick him out of the house with conditions, but the son will still be the son.

Acts 1:25

"That he may take part of this ministry and apostleship, from which Judas through his transgression fell, that he might go to his own place."

Statement of temporary salvation: It is implied here that Judas, one of the twelve apostles, was a born-again believer, and then it is stated that, because of his transgressions of being a traitor to his faith, that he fell and lost that salvation.

Statement of permanent salvation: Nowhere in the Bible does it ever state, nor is it ever completely clear, that Judas was a "believer" Christian having made a complete and total commitment to Christ in following him. Judas, of course, could not have been born-again because the ability to make this commitment did not come until the Day of Pentecost, after Christ's death. Many of the above verses stated in this chapter (much like Acts 1:25) have made the incorrect assumption the person or persons related to the text were saved to begin with.

I Timothy 4:1

"Now the Spirit speaks expressly, that in the latter times some shall depart from the faith, giving heed to seducing spirits, and false doctrines of devils;"

Statement of temporary salvation: As we draw nearer and nearer to the second coming of Christ, some people will depart from their faith in God (as believer Christians) so much so that they will lose their salvation. This will be caused by the seducing spirits of Satan and doctrines of evil.

Statement of permanent salvation: It is true that as we near to the second coming of Christ, some people will fall away from the level of inspiration and vigor as compared to their first spiritual love in Christ Jesus. It won't be as much they have become agnostic or atheistic in their views as it will be that they have lost that initial motivation to please God and study hard to understand and execute His will in their lives; relating to the original passion they once had. They will become useless vessels so that God will be unable to use them according to His will and, therefore, reach a point in their life where they stagnate, stop growing in the Lord, and become spiritually useless according to the gifts and talents they were given by God to witness to others and to demonstrate Christ-like love to others. Satan can deceive people and render their Christian walk ineffective leading them into continued sin. Their salvation is not necessarily lost, however. In those situations, they become like any other Christian who falls into sin or is living a life contrary to God's expectation of them, differing again only in degrees of infraction. We have been given an example by God how to love others (as demonstrated by Jesus), and it is our challenge to live as close to that expectation as possible according to what we are convicted to do, knowing full well that it is impossible to live perfect according to our actions, deeds, and just as importantly, our motives and thoughts.

It is also probable that I Timothy 4:1 refers to a person who is not, and never has been in Christ and therefore cannot be used according to God's purpose and perfect Will according to his spiritual potential as a human being. I Peter 1:20 tells us that God foreordained people before the foundation of the world to become born-again and be saved. There are many who were preordained to, through time, never accept Christ as their Savior and become saved. This is not saying that each person does not have a choice as a free moral agent. It is only saying that God knew before the world was created who would accept His free gift in Jesus and who would not. Several chapters later from I Timothy 4:1, we are told in II Timothy 3:13 that evil men and seducers will become worse and worse, deceiving, and being deceived (by Satan). There is no mention in or around this verse in II Timothy which tells us that these seducers were once born-again and saved.

Looking at Romans 7, even the apostle Paul, as a born-again believer, was unable to keep from sinning. He tried not to do the things he knew he shouldn't do but sometimes couldn't help himself. The sin inside him was so strong that it sometimes overcame him and when he wanted to do right he struggled, sometimes slipped and did things that were wrong. As a true person in Christ, his new life told him to do right, but the sin-nature was still inside him trying to make him sin. Paul tells us what a terrible predicament he was in. At the end of these verses, Paul rejoices in knowing that he has a great Mediator, the person of the Lord Jesus Christ, who has made him perfect in the eyes of God in spite all of his sins, and that he has a Holy Comforter (the Holy Spirit) to guide him in love to his fellow man and to the will of God. Because of this, we are told in Romans 8:1 that there is no longer any condemnation to those who are in Christ and death (receiving the punishment for unbelief) no longer has dominion over him – and all believers in Christ.

James 5:9

"Grudge not one against another, brethren, lest you be condemned: behold, the judge stands before the door."

Statement of temporary salvation: If we hold a grudge against one another we will be condemned and lose our salvation.

Statement of permanent salvation: The preceding verses to 5:9 tell us that every man is tempted and that we should always be slow to wrath (James 1:14,19). James 4:11 tells us that we are not to judge one another because we cheapen God's Law of Love. James 2:10-13 tells us that whoever keeps the whole law but offends in one small part is guilty of the entire law. We are also, according to these verses, not to pick and choose which sins we feel are graver than others, say for example anger being worse than lying. If we do that we are to be judged with no mercy. There is also evidence in James 3:1-3 that would lead one to believe that James 5:9 (the object of this discussion) is speaking about people who are unsaved.

II Peter 1:9,10

"But he that lacks these things is blind, and cannot see afar off, and has forgotten that he was purged from his old sins. Wherefore the rather, brethren, give diligence to make your calling and election sure: for if you do these things, ye shall never fall:"

Statement of temporary salvation: It is assumed that, if we ever forget the sins that we were purged from that we will fall, and falling means we will lose our salvation and our election will not be sure.

Statement of permanent salvation: II Peter was written to give its readers hope in terms of their apprehension concerning an afterlife. In terms of the phrase "if you do these things", who is to determine how much is to be done? Falling doesn't necessarily mean losing salvation. I Peter 1:3-5 and I Peter 1:13-16 both tell us that we have a great hope by the resurrection of Christ from the dead to a perfect and enduring spiritual inheritance, and a salvation that doesn't fade away and is kept by God. Everyone falls. It is discouraging and pessimistic without hope if we choose to view someone falling in the Christina walk as necessarily losing their salvation.

Conclusion

I John 5:13 tells us that if we believe on the name of Christ, we should know we will have eternal life. Eternal means having no end, continuing without interruption, and forever true and changeless. Assurance of salvation means to be absolutely confident we are saved and if death should occur, we would be in Heaven (John 10:27-29, 5:24, and 6:47). Anyone who believes on Christ as their Savior is entitled to this eternal assurance (John 1:12, 3:16, and 3:36).

Galatians 4:6 tells us that the Holy Spirit witnesses to us that we are indeed saved and provides needed assurances. Additionally, John 5:24, Acts 13:39, and Romans 10:13 tell us that permanence in our salvation is promised to us. Essentially, the only commitment God wants from us at the time we surrender to Him and accept Christ as our Savior is that of a total and full commitment. He does not want and will not accept anything less. As we see Him as a perfect and Holy God, we would expect nothing less from Him.

Christ tells us we are to love one another as we would ourselves and that what we do to the least of His we do to Him. This "agape" love in the New Testament is best characterized by unconditional love that we are to give to others without expectation that they would give back to us in return. This is the same unconditional love that God extends to us if we are truly saved and under the redemptive grace of Christ's death, burial, and resurrection. Even if we are truly born-again Christians, we will continue to fail at following the commandment that Christ gave to us of loving our neighbor as ourselves. Certainly, we will have a much better chance of coming closer to Christ's expectation of us in terms of loving others, but we will still fall short. The Holy Spirit will guide us and direct us, but we will still fail in terms of not being able to be completely perfect through our actions and works. Fortunately, we have already been made spiritually pure and white as snow at the time we accepted Christ as our Savior. We have been given an example by God how to love others (as demonstrated by Jesus), and it is our challenge (by our choices) to live as close to that expectation as possible, knowing full well that it is impossible to always live perfect according to our actions, deeds, and just as importantly, our motives and thoughts.

Christ did the entire job of offering Himself for us in the most perfect and total manner. Nothing else had to be (or has to) done besides accepting that gift (Hebrews 5:8-10, 10:10-12, John 19:30). So, if we did not save ourselves by our great works and deeds, whatever would make us believe that we would be able to maintain that salvation through works and deeds (as is stated in Romans and Galatians). Especially since these outward works are not truly representative, under many circumstances, of who we are inside, what our internal motivations are, and what our heart's desires truly are (Romans 7:7).

Many people believe that at the time they are saved, the only sins that are forgiven in their lives are those they have committed in their past, and that any sins they commit in their future will need to be granted forgiveness of again and again, after they confess them. The question can be asked however: At the time of Christ's death (the purpose of which was to completely forgive and take away all the sins of the world) how many of our sins were in the future? The answer to this is that of course all of them were. This means that all our sins (past and future) are forgiven at the time of our acceptance of salvation because they were all "future sins" at the time of Christ's death, the object of all of our faith. The reason this is so important is that the proponents of salvation being temporary (until such time as we sin) often times adhere to this "past only" philosophy of forgiveness. Salvation is permanent as is God's love for us and as our responsibility to love others will always be.

<u>Salvation being permanent is never a license to sin and use that freedom as a permit to do whatever we want to do</u>. To the contrary, the security, peace and unconditional love we receive from God through this permanence of salvation is intended for us

to realize our true spiritual potential in Christ as we are guided by the Holy Spirit to love others more fully and to not abuse or take advantage of that freedom in any way. This topic will be more fully explored and discussed in greater detail in the chapter entitled The Grace Message.

Reflection & Study Questions For This Chapter:

- Because we are saved, does this mean we will never sin?
- Why is it so important for us to know that salvation is permanent?
- This chapter examined 21 Scripture verses in the context of how each verse has been used to justify temporary salvation, including apologetics for those justifications. For you, which Scripture was most impactful in terms of supporting the concept that salvation is permanent?
- For those who believe salvation is permanent, could there be a temptation to use this assurance and security to sin more?

Chapter 4

The Grace Message

The law, primarily consisting of the Ten Commandments, was the operating principle in the Old Covenant. It was also the vehicle for our communication with God. In the New Covenant, grace (based on God's love for us) is the operating principle and is the way we communicate with Him through self-spiritual growth and loving others. God's message of grace to us consists of many aspects (for lack of a better word). In addition to certain amazing events and effects of those events, grace partially consists of God's definition of love as outlined in I Corinthians 13 and the fruits of His Spirit as outlined in Galatians 5 and 6. Although the entire Bible includes God's perfect plan for humanity, and it is understood the New Testament builds on the Old Testament (the New Covenant building on the Old Covenant), the grace message is separate from, and in some instances, opposite of, the Old Covenant Law as outlined in the Ten Commandments.

Grace is loving, giving, selfless, good willed and merciful and includes a tremendous outlook of humility as well as a willingness to pardon and forgive others for things they do wrong. Grace is also a favor or freedom rendered by someone who doesn't have to provide that favor to another. It is an unmerited favor and is a wonderful gift someone gives to us, and one we can give to another. Grace is the essence of love and under it, the Holy Spirit directs and completely empowers as He guides and equips us. To the extent we can remove ourselves as being an obstacle to His leading, He can guide us. Through this guidance, we can be our best according to God's expectations for us. The "Grace Message" primarily consists of the following 'aspects' as found in Scripture. They are not listed in any specific order and do not exist in isolation from each other but instead are interconnected, and dependent upon each other:

Aspect # 1

As discussed in the previous chapter, Christian salvation is permanent and knowing this, born again believers can be completely thankful and confident in the completeness of Christ's death on the Cross for them and therefore, can be fully committed in living in the grace and unconditional love God has for them. With this permanent salvation, and not having to spend energy always looking back and wondering about their "standing" with God, Christians should then be focused on engaging themselves completely in the full responsibility to live their lives unencumbered or uninhibited to glorify God's name with their unconditional love towards others.

Aspect # 2

The complete and total forgiveness we receive by God and through Christ's death at the Cross is critical, but it is only half of the salvation message. The other half is Christ's resurrection and Him living inside each believer in the form of the Holy Spirit which permanently indwells inside us and guiding as we love others.

Aspect # 3

The finality of Christ's sacrifice on the Cross means complete and unconditional love and forgiveness to the believer with no requirement to ask God for forgiveness each time there is sin. Along with this, and stemming from that unconditional love we experience from God, is the aspect of demonstrating unconditional love for others. This does not mean we have unconditional love for all their behaviors, but it does mean that we love them for who they are separate from those behaviors which may be inconsistent with God's word.

Aspect # 4

Guided by the Holy Spirit, we are to follow the only commandment given by God under the New Covenant: to love one another with all of who we are. This commandment is given to us in multiple parts of Scripture including John 13:34,35, John 15:12 and I Corinthians 13. Fortunately, God has not only provided a perfect example of what this means (as seen in the love that Christ demonstrated through his life, death and resurrection), but He provides us ample instruction and description as to what Grace and love means (I Corinthians 13 and Galatians 5&6).

Aspect # 5

The understanding we are to live in the Spirit after we are saved along with living up to the amazing responsibility that comes with this freedom. Continually sinning after we are saved is inconsistent with our new nature in Christ and the indwelling of the Holy Spirit inside us. Out of the love we constantly receive from God through the spiritual knowledge we have by becoming born-again, we are more acutely aware of God's expectations of us using our gifts and talents to glorify Him through our genuine and complete love towards others.

Aspect # 6

The realization that we have a personal relationship with God and that, although there are many similarities in what our Christian walks should look like as a body of believers, each individual Christian relationship with God is completely unique from another's.

Aspect # 7

Discussed in a later chapter, understanding that our prayers have several purposes some of which are: a.) For us to accept, trust and believe in His perfect will for us which he is already aware of;

b.) For us to realize the full extent of God's grace and love that He has already given to us as a Christian, and c.) For us to individually be more convicted through meditation with His Holy Spirit which resides in us as to how we should love others.

Aspect # 8

With great acceptance and peace, having a full understanding that blessings we receive from God not only take the form of things that go right for us or make us happy in the moment but that also, that we are fully blessed when things don't go the way we want; even when tremendous difficulties are present.

Except for aspects which have already been discussed at length in the previous chapter, or will be discussed in the chapter called "Prayer", each of these will be examined here in greater detail:

Aspect # 1

Christian salvation is permanent and knowing this, born again believers can be completely thankful and confident in the completeness of Christ's death on the Cross for them and therefore, can be fully committed in living in the grace and unconditional love God has for them. With this permanent salvation, and not having to spend energy always looking back and wondering about their "standing" with God, Christians should then be completely focused and concerned about engaging themselves one hundred percent in the full responsibility to live their lives unencumbered or uninhibited to glorify God's name with their unconditional love towards others.

Aspect # 2

The complete forgiveness we receive by God and through Christ is critical, but it is only half of the salvation message. The other half is Christ's resurrection and Him living inside each believer in the form of the Holy Spirit which permanently indwells inside us; and guides us.

We realize that the first important step in entering Christian salvation is recognizing and admitting we have a sin nature before God and because of that sin nature, we need some way to make us spiritually pure in the eyes of a perfect God. The New Covenant requires us to trust in the saving and finished act of Christ at the Cross. Philippians 3:9 states that we should be found in him, not having our own righteousness based on the Law, but instead through the faith of Christ, the righteousness which is of God by faith.

Forgiveness by God, through Christ, is only half of the message of salvation. The other half is accepting and living in Christ's resurrected life so His priority for our lives can be realized through us allowing the Holy Spirit to fully guide our hearts as He indwells in us. Until we completely rest in the finality of what Christ did at the Cross and the forgiveness we received from that act, we will never experience the full truth and life of the resurrection – and the full importance of allowing the risen Christ, through the Holy Spirit, to live in us daily. It is completely amazing to me that the word "hope" is virtually never used in the New Testament while Christ was living but was used over 70 times after his death. The significance of this is not understood until we realize that Christ stated He would have to go away (his life ending) before the Holy Comforter (Holy Spirit) would be able to come to this earth and live inside each believer. The "hope" then is in Christ's death and the dynamic which followed which was that, with Christ gone, the Hoy Spirit was then "eligible" to permanently indwell in us to guide us and give us complete hope.

I Corinthians 15:13-17 tells us that if there is no resurrection of the dead, then Christ is not risen and if Christ did not rise from the dead, then our preaching and our Gospel is in vain, and therefore our faith. Because, if Christ was not raised from the dead by God, your faith is in vain, because the Holy Spirit is not able to indwell in the believer and have hope to conquer sin in their life. Romans 6:5-8 states we have been planted together in the likeness of his death; we should also completely identify and be in the likeness of His life through His resurrection. Our 'old man' (old sin nature) then is crucified with him, that the body of sin might be destroyed, that from now on, we should not serve sin. For he that is dead is freed from sin. If the controlling aspects of our sin nature dies at the time of our salvation (renders us in Christ), we can have full faith that we should also live (and be fully alive) with him. Man's identification with God through Christ cannot occur fully until we realize we are raised with Him through faith and that Christ is alive in our hearts in the form of the Holy Spirit. This is why in baptism the preacher completely submerges the believer all the way under the water symbolizing being buried under the ground and then being lifted up above the ground (analogous to the water).

Colossians 2:11-14 continues this point: We are buried with him in baptism and are raised with him through the faith of the operation of God, who has raised him from the dead. And you, being dead in your sins and the impureness of your flesh, he has made the believer alive together with him, having forgiven all trespasses; erasing the handwriting of ordinances that was against us, which was contrary to us, and took it out of the way, nailing it to his Cross. I Peter 1:3,4 tells us that according to God's abundant mercy, He has established us again to a lively hope by the resurrection of Jesus from the dead to an inheritance incorruptible, and undefiled, and one that does not fade away, reserved in Heaven for you. We are reconciled with God and saved through not only the death of His Son but also through His life in us as Christians (Romans 5:10). Death is said to have entered the world by Adam's transgression, but life is obtained by receiving the free gift from Christ.

Romans 5:17,18 tells us that through Adam's disobedience, death came into the world but also by one (Christ) we can receive abundant grace and the gift of righteousness. Therefore, as by the offence of one judgment came upon all men to condemnation; even so by the righteousness of one the free gift came upon all men unto justification of life. According to Paul in Ephesians 2:4-5, we were dead in our sins, but we are made alive in Christ: But God, who is rich in mercy, for his great love where he loved us, even when we were dead in sins, has quickened us together with Christ, (by God's grace we become saved).

As we live with the Holy Spirit inside us, we are to always bear witness of the Holy Spirit and not ourselves. This means making choices which reflect our spiritual nature (and its desires) yielding to the workings of the Holy Spirit in us. The versus in the table below outline this extremely important Biblical principle:

I Corinthians 1:19-2:16	God will make foolish the wisdom of the wise and the wisdom of this world. He will make foolish the intelligence of the intelligent. God chooses the week things of the world to shame the strong. We are not to come to people in our own eloquence and superior wisdom but instead reference the Holy Spirit as our power in humility. The best way we can know the thoughts of a man is to know the man's spirit within him. We have not received the spirit of the world but the Spirit of God.
John 5:30-32	By ourselves, we can do nothing. By my thoughts and actions, I am challenged to honor God who sent me. If I testify of myself, my testimony is not valid. It is only valid when my testimony reflects the Holy Spirit which is inside me.
John 7:16-18 & 8:54	Jesus states that his teaching is not his own but from God. He who speaks on his own does so to honor himself but he who works for the honor of the one who sent him speaks the truth.

John 15:4	No branch can bear fruit by itself. Our Christian walk is only as powerful as how much we allow the Holy Spirit inside us to guide our actions.
Acts 3:11-16	Peter proclaims that it is not the human power he has that has healed this person; instead, it is the power of the Holy Spirit inside him.
I Corinthians 3:16	We are God's temple and God's Holy Spirit lives inside each Christian.
Romans 12:1	We are to offer our bodies as living sacrifices, holy and pleasing to God. As Christians, this is our spiritual act of worship.

Along with this challenge is the concept that our good deeds should always be fruits of our inner faith. That said, we should not do "good things" in this world which end up keeping us from the "best things". Multiple versus in the books of James and Galatians testify to the truth of this. Baba Dioum said: "In the end, we will conserve only what we love; We will love only what we understand; We will understand only what we are taught." Relating this line of thinking to our Christian walk, it can be said that we will only love others to the same degree we feel we are loved unconditionally by God; we will only forgive others to the same degree we feel we are forgiven by God; and we will only give hope to others to the same degree we feel we have hope from God.

Aspect # 3:

The finality of Christ's sacrifice on the Cross means complete and unconditional love and forgiveness to the believer with no requirement to ask God for forgiveness each time the person sins. Along with this, and stemming from that unconditional love we experience from God, is the aspect of demonstrating unconditional love for others. This does not mean we have unconditional love for all their behaviors, but it does mean that we love them for who they are separate from those behaviors which may at times be inconsistent with God's word.

One of the descriptions God gives concerning how to love each other is that we should not keep track or a record of each other's faults and mistakes (I Corinthians 13:5, Galatians 5:22-23, and Colossians 3:12-14). Since how God tells us to love each other is a model as to how Christ loves us, including how God loves us by giving us His Son to die for us, it's clear that God does not keep track of our faults, mistakes, and transgressions. Therefore, after we have become a Christian, God no longer keeps track and a record of our wrongdoings where He would allow it to influence our position and identity as His son or daughter. If He did, this would be God controlling us through conditions on our actions and motivating to do things (or not do things) based on guilt (and basically bringing back the doctrines of the Old Covenant). God's banner over us in the New Covenant is love and grace, not fear and guilt. It happens all too often in our world where relationships and influence in those relationships is based on guilt and a dysfunctional misuse of power. God does not do this with us. Our relationship with Him is based on something much healthier and more positive which lifts us up to our potential as He sees in us; not caged up and limited by guilt and conditions on His love for us. All too often, control by others (based on their own insecurities and misunderstanding of what God's grace means) is a driving force for inflicting guilt on others. Then, through the years and based in their families and churches, people get so used to staying away from sin because they are being watched closely by the elders, church leadership and/or many others in the church, that there is no capacity built into the believer based on an independent individualistic personal relationship with Christ; it is all based on how much I should stay within the lines of what others have established and how they perceive me.

This is very sad since the amazing and unique gifts and individualistic ministries by each person are quelled and covered up so they are unable to completely flourish and abound. People sometimes get so used to living under this kind of "guidance" of others that they have no clue as to how to live according to the freedom and unbridled power that God gives to them as believer Christians. Instead, Satan wins by people perverting the freedom and grace of God's word as "willing victims" and are all too willing to passively follow the leadership and the majority out of fear and a desire to be included in the church "fellowship". In the field of psychology, there is a term called "co-dependent relationship" and it basically means that one person engages in dysfunctional acts to maintain a relationship with another person who is also engaging in dysfunctional acts. They enable each other. The actions of each are symbiotic (they need each other to survive). Analogous to the above example, there are many church leaders who dysfunctionally love having control over others. It is based on personal insecurity in them and satisfies a deep part inside them, but it is not healthy and is not consistent with Christian principles of personal accountability and the full use of each person's gifts. Conversely, there are all too many followers in our churches who are more than willing to be controlled by these people I have mentioned. It's almost as if they have sought out a system of Christian religion (that they have found in their church) which satisfies their deep desires to be controlled by others so they don't have to take personal responsibility for their own spiritual life and so they don't have to take any "risk" by trying to rise to God's personal challenge to them. They choose to be followers. Therefore, they are unable to "eat the meat" of God's word and assume the full spiritual growth God has prepared for them but instead, are satisfied just drinking baby's milk their entire lives through followership. Finally on this point, many of these church members and leaders are more worried about their "cup" being clean on the outside (as an outward appearance to others) than they are to see the filth on the inside of their cup which often only God can see. Their behaviors are hypocritical, and they only fool themselves as they believe that no one notices and realizes it (Christian and non-Christian alike).

A friend of mine once had a car that had a broken speedometer. Every time I got in the car, I always looked over to see if he had gotten it fixed but he never had. Finally, one day I asked him:

"How do you drive your car without getting into an accident with no speedometer." His answer amazed me. He said: "I just drive according to the road conditions. If it's raining, I slow down to a very safe speed. If it's a highway, I drive a little bit slower than the rest of the traffic. If I'm taking a corner, going over a hill or taking a curve, I slow down to a very safe speed." If we assume for a minute that the speedometer is analogous to the Old Covenant law and rigid requirements, it can be seen that (although the Motor Vehicle Administration does require it) we can drive a car safely and with no accidents without relying on a speedometer. Similarly, we can (and should) live a full and very meaningful Christian life without rigidly adhering to the Ten Commandments and the laws established by many over-controlling churches and their leadership.

After someone has become a born-again Christian, walking church aisles on Sundays to gain forgiveness and to make a public statement of an intention to "get back into friendship with God", acts of repentance to God, and attending confession booths – all have no place in God's grace message, and are not consistent with what God teaches us in His Word about our permanent standing in His eyes. <u>Actions such as these cheapen the completed work of Christ at the Cross and the finality of confession to God and forgiveness of our sins based on our belief of the shed blood of Christ at the Cross and acceptance of the free gift of salvation</u>. Just as important, actions such as these also use up valuable emotional and physical energy that is better used in service to others and in doing God's work. Also, and very important, sometimes there is a tendency for people to ask God to forgive them and then they feel they don't have to go to the person who may have been offended by their actions, since they have already asked forgiveness from God. This is counter to what the Bible teaches.

As born-again Christians, there can be no condemnation towards us because Christ paid for our sins completely once and for all. Sins and iniquities, (past, present, and future), are no longer remembered by God, as outlined in the following verses (italics mine): There is therefore *no condemnation* to them which are in Christ (Romans 8:1). We are sanctified through the offering of Jesus, *once for all* (Hebrews 10:10).

The Bible tells us that without the shedding of blood there can be no forgiveness of sins. With the sacrifice of Christ at the Cross of Calvary, God established a method whereby mankind could enter God's perfect and pure presence in Heaven by accepting Christ as his Savior – as a mediator between God and man. The reason for this is that we become spiritually pure at the time of our salvation due to the finished work of Christ. In terms of our soul and body, our entire lifetime is spent being perfected but spiritually, Christ's blood has made us spiritually perfect. Christ was sent to die for the sins of man once. His death took away sins forever for those who would believe on His name. If we believe we must continually ask God to forgive us of our sins we are, in essence, asking God to send Christ back down to earth to be crucified for those future sins – or some other sacrifice. The reason this must be true is because we know the Bible tells us that without the shedding of blood, there can be no forgiveness or remission of sins.

As mentioned earlier, in the Old Testament, the Day of Atonement was the time where sins were "covered" (or temporarily eliminated until the following year) by the sacrifices of bulls and goats. Sins were not taken away, they were merely covered. In the New Testament, <u>the word atonement is never even used</u> because Christ, as sent by God, did not come to cover sins; he came to completely take them away. This is stated in Hebrews 10:17,18 and Romans 6:9,10 where God tells us the new believer's sins and iniquities *will be remembered no more*. Now, where remission of these is, there is *no more offering for sin*. Knowing that Christ, being raised from the dead, dies no more and that death has no more dominion over him. For in that he died, *he died unto sin once for all time*. Perfection could not be achieved through the Old Covenant with man. The New Covenant, however, establishes a method whereby man can be justified, sanctified and made perfect spiritually forever in the eyes of God as is written in Hebrews 10:14 that by one offering he has *perfected for ever* them that are sanctified by the free gift of salvation.

Christ's death took away all sins of the world, including the ones which had not occurred at the time of His death, but would occur in the future. I Peter 3:18 states: For Christ has *once suffered for sins*, the just for the unjust, that he might bring us to God, being put to death in the flesh, but made alive by the Spirit. Hebrews 9:26 states: Christ has *appeared to put away sin* by the sacrifice of himself. John 1:29 tells us that after the death of Jesus, John saw Him coming towards him, and said, Behold the Lamb of God, which *takes away the sin of the world*. John 5:24 states: "He that hears my word, and believes on him that sent me, has everlasting life, and *shall not come into condemnation*; but is passed from death unto life." (Italics mine)

In the Old Covenant, the priest would enter the Holy of Holies (tabernacle) to repeatedly offer sacrifices for the sins of the people. In the New Covenant however, Christ came to offer Himself up only once for mankind. Hebrews 9:25,28 tells us that Christ will not offer himself often, as the high priest enters the holy place every year with the blood of others as occurred in the Old Covenant. Christ was offered by God to bear the sins of many only once (Hebrews 9:12). I John 3:5 tells us that Jesus took away our sins forever, and didn't just cover them for a time. Hebrews 8:12 and 10:12 tell us that God, through Christ, offered *one sacrifice for sins forever* and that *their sins and iniquities He will remember no more.*

In becoming born again spiritually, the life we have is everlasting. Everlasting does not mean until the next time we sin; it means eternal duration; forever. John 3:16 tells us that God loved the world so much that he gave His only Son that whoever would believe in him would not perish, but have life forever. Our sins are completely taken away and nailed to the Cross (Colossians 2:13-14) and God has made us alive into the New Covenant in Christ and forgiven all our trespasses. Colossians continues by saying that Christ *took the legalistic ordinances out of the way and nailed them to his Cross.* John 10:28 assures us that Christ has given us eternal life and those who have Him as their Savior will never perish nor be taken out of the protective hands of God. John 6:35 tells us that Jesus exclaims He is the bread of life and anyone who believes in Him will never hunger or thirst spiritually. Once Christ is in us, we are to rest from our own works to obtain salvation, and righteousness in the sight of God (Hebrews 4:9-11).

As an instructor and manager having been involved in leadership and supervisory training for over 25 years, I have seen many people be promoted into senior executive positions. For reasons I believe that are based on conformity, inclusion, and a misguided definition of competence, they seem to be drawn towards making decisions and behaving in ways they think a senior executive should behave and make decisions. In other words, even though data and their gut may tell them to make one decision or take a certain action, they are guided more by what they believe society or their organization believes are "executive type decision making" or "executive type actions". I believe this same dynamic is true among Christian leaders and pastors of today in churches that include unnecessary aspects of legalism. They believe the expectation for them (and all elders) is to keep track of others' faults and monitor the level of holiness each person has in the church so they can step in and impart their own sense of righteousness and perfect guidance on them. Unfortunately, they see this as their legitimate role and if they were not to do this, they would be derelict in their role and responsibilities.

Believing on the name of Christ means we have spiritual rest in that Christ did it all and there is nothing left for us to do to earn our way to Heaven. Once we have taken Christ as our Savior, our record of sin is cleared, as stated in Hebrews 1:1-3 (paraphrased); God, who spoke to us in the past through the prophets, has recently spoken to us through Jesus. Jesus died to cleanse us and clear our record of all sin. As born-again Christians, we have a new life which lasts forever, not one passed onto us by our parents, for the life they gave us will some day be gone. It is a spiritual life and one which will last for all time because it comes from Christ. Hebrews 9:15 tells us that we have a permanent and eternal inheritance in Christ.

Some believe we still need to keep our record clean with God by constantly asking Him for forgiveness as was expected in the Old Covenant Law. The most common verse cited to support this way of thinking is I John 1:9. I John 1:9 states that: "If we confess our sins, God is faithful to forgive us our sins and to cleanse us from all unrighteousness." Many incorrectly believe this verse was written to the believer and justifies the need to constantly ask God for forgiveness. However, this verse was written to the unbeliever and therefore it was not speaking to believers who were to "get right with God" after they sinned. In I John, John was writing to the Gnostics who believed that first, Jesus did not come in the flesh and second, we were not born with a sin nature. John is the type of person who is very direct so he gets right to the focus of his writing in I John 1:1 where he states: We have heard and have seen with our eyes, which we have looked upon and our hands have handled. This was referring to Jesus and was clearly making the point that Jesus did in fact come in the flesh. Also, I John 4:2 tells us that every spirit that confesses that Jesus came in the flesh is of God. John then moves to the second issue of the sin nature. He states in I John 1:8 that if we say we have no sin (sin nature) we are deceiving ourselves and when we deceive ourselves, the Truth is therefore not in us (the literal truth and Christ as Truth). Later in the 3rd chapter, we see clearly that the word truth refers only to believing on the name of Christ as Savior. (I John 3:23)

I John 1:10 states: If we say we haven't sinned, then we make Him out to be a liar, and His Word is not in us. Basically, this means that if we say we don't have a sin nature and therefore we don't believe we need Jesus as Savior to deal with that sin nature, His Word (which is the Truth with a capital "T") is not in us. Further, I John 2:22 states: A person who is a liar is any person who denies that Jesus is the Christ, and therefore has never made the choice to be saved. Additionally, I John 2: 3, 4 says: We know God if we keep His commandments and whoever does not keep his commandments is a liar and the Truth is not in Him. These are not the Ten Commandments. We know this because I John 3: 23 says: His Commandment is that we should believe on the name of His Son Jesus Christ and love one another. So this commandment relates to believing on the name of Christ as our Savior <u>because</u> we have a sin nature, and then once we are born again and indwelt with that Spirit, we are then equipped and empowered to be able to love one another according to how our own personal relationship with Christ provides. Finally, I John 4: 20, 21 says: If a person says I love God and hates his brother, he is a liar for he who does not love his brother who he has seen; how can he love God who He has not seen? And the commandment we have from Him is basic and foundational: that he who loves God must love his brother as well.

Although it is not necessary to ask God's forgiveness under the New Covenant, under grace, forgiveness should be asked from others if we have offended them. This forgiveness between men is to take precedence over worship to God (Matt. 5) and should always reflect the love and forgiveness we receive from God (Matt. 5:7, 6:12-15, 7:1-5 & 18). It should be an example of God's love for us (Matt. 5) and a reflection of how we want to be forgiven from others when we make mistakes and transgress (Matt. 7). This forgiveness and spirit of non-judgment we show towards others is an example as we witness to lead others to Christ as well. We have not only been given the power to forgive again and again, but also the duty (Luke 17:3-4).

At the time of our salvation, God says: "There are no more actions you need to do. You are already made justified in the eyes of God by your belief in the finished work of Jesus Christ. What you have already done by accepting my Son as your Savior is all you need to do – plus nothing!

Aspect # 4:

Guided by the Holy Spirit, we are inspired to follow the only commandment given by God under the New Covenant. This is to love one another with all of who we are empowered by how well we can operate unhindered by our carnal desires and for us to be driven by the Holy Spirit in Christ. This commandment is in various Scripture including John 13:34,35, John 15:12 and I Corinthians 13. Fortunately, God has not only provided a perfect example of what this means, as seen in the love that Christ demonstrated through his life and death, but He provides us ample instruction and description as to what grace and love actually mean. These are described in the books of I Corinthians and Galatians as outlined below. Before we review these characteristics in grace towards others, and for which we are to possess in our hearts, we understand it is not possible unless we fully realize we cannot demonstrate pure selfless "agape" love apart from Jesus and the guiding Holy Spirit which indwells in us (John 15:5).

I Corinthians 13 tells us that love:

- ☐ Is patient and kind;
- ☐ Is not envious of others;
- ☐ Is not proud and puffed up;
- ☐ Is not self-seeking;
- ☐ Is not easily angered;
- ☐ Keeps no record of wrongs;
- ☐ Does not rejoice in evil but delights in the truth;
- ☐ Always protects those who are weaker;
- ☐ Always trusts;
- ☐ Always hopes;
- ☐ Always remains steadfast, perseveres and never fails;

Galatians 5 & 6 tells us that the fruits of the Spirit in our lives are:

- ☐ Love and Joy
- ☐ Peace
- ☐ Patience
- ☐ Kindness
- ☐ Goodness
- ☐ Faithfulness
- ☐ Gentleness
- ☐ Self-control
- ☐ Not being envious
- ☐ Not provoking
- ☐ Not being conceited
- ☐ Not being proud and puffed up

Placed side by side, the similarity in how God defines love and describes the fruits of the Spirit can be more readily seen:

Characteristic / Quality	I Corinthians 13 (Defines love)	Galatians 5 & 6 (Fruits of the Spirit)
Patient and kind	✓	✓
Not envious of others	✓	✓
Not proud and puffed up	✓	✓
Is not self seeking	✓	✓
Is not easily angered	✓	✓
Keeps no records of wrong	✓	
Does not rejoice in evil but delights in the truth	✓	✓
Always protects those who are weaker	✓	✓
Always trusts	✓	✓
Always hopes	✓	✓
Always remains steadfast, perseveres and never fails	✓	

Almost without exception, all the characteristics which God uses to define love outlined in I Corinthians are also included in the fruits of the Spirit in Galatians. Where there isn't an obvious overlap, these characteristics are implicit in the others. One important aspect of loving others, and the attitude we should have with the selfless "agape" love as demonstrated by Christ as a precursor to the advent of the New Covenant, relates to the issue of pride and humility. Under grace, we have a tremendous responsibility to have a humble heart and to move away from pride. The only way we can approach others with the proper focus on taking care of their needs over our own is if we have a humble heart. This is only possible if we remember that we cannot demonstrate agape love apart from Christ and His Holy Spirit which always resides in us. We are a new creation, and we are then in Christ (II Corinthians 5:17). Romans 14 tells us to focus on things that establish an atmosphere of peace with others and in encouraging them to grow in their Christian walk. In action, this includes but is not limited to:

☐ Demonstrating our true servant hood to others as stated in John 13:14-16 and Acts 1:35. More often than not, what this actually means is meeting people where they are and where their needs exist according to the personal nature of their own unique circumstances. Once we are aware of the needs of others and are convicted to serve them, servant hood takes the form of meeting needs and wants of another person without any expectation of thanks or appreciation. In this situation, the sin nature which still indwells in us, expects thanks and appreciation whereas the spiritual nature has its reward just by the attitude and act of giving at the time it occurs. Part of this also includes key points in II Corinthians 9 where we are told to give of ourselves completely and cheerfully. With this, we can approach others with the attitude that God has already made us sufficient in all things, has given us complete peace knowing all our needs are taken care of and therefore, we can approach others with this same attitude of peace, certainty, and grace.

- [ ] Having a meek and approachable spirit as stated in Romans 10:9-13. Sometimes as Christians, we say we are approachable and have an 'open door policy' to others but in reality, we walk around with chips on our shoulders one step away from being short tempered, overly rigid and stubborn, or so intense that we push others away before they can even get near us. The Bible tells us that a kind gentle word turns away wrath. If God's wonderful Spirit lives inside us and we are guided by His love, we can work very hard to consciously send out signals to others that we are approachable and meek with kindness and understanding. <u>In this way, we are a better ambassador for God and we are more able to walk our talk with spiritual integrity allowing God's love to be seen in our eyes, words, tone of voice, countenance and our entire demeanor.</u> In this context, we should always be asking ourselves an extremely important question: How far away is a smile from our countenance? If the light is truly in us, it is important for us to show that light in our smile. <u>Others should see the joy of God on our faces, especially in times of difficulty.</u> We are to demonstrate the tremendous hope and joy we have in Christ each day on this earth. With so many carnal distractions and problems, this is much easier said than done but God's word encourages us for this.

- [ ] Consistent with this, but directed specifically to non-believers, II Timothy 2:24,25 tells us not to quarrel but to be gentle to all, having the ability to teach others with patience and in great humility, to teach others who are unsaved through modeling the way.

- [ ] Not judging other's heart and their standing as a Christian while simultaneously striving to balance this with confronting a fellow Christian in love, grace and humility as we challenge their walk according to the expectation, security and peace they have from and in God (John 8:7).

- ☐ Not being hypocritical but instead, walking with spiritual integrity and humility and according to God's high standard for us. Romans 12:9-17 not only reminds us of our responsibility to not be hypocritical but also tells us to be devoted to one another in brotherly love, to honor one another, to be fervent in spirit, to be of the same mind in Christ as one another, and to not be prideful.

- ☐ And, as it relates to the humility of our own actions as well as the actions of others, for us to always be asking: "Who gets the glory?" The answer to this should always be God, Jesus, the Holy Spirit (who leads us) and/or others in our life. James 4:6 tells us that God opposes the proud but gives grace to the humble. This can be constant encouragement for us to leave our pride behind and embrace humility in all we do. The only way this is possible is if we realize we are trying to impress God and not ourselves or those in this world. The only way it is possible is that if we continually realize we are dependent on God's Holy Spirit to help us understand not only how to love others but also how to place pride in its proper place as subservient to the lifting up of others. The only pride we should ever have is the pride we have as to what we have been blessed with by God through our salvation in Christ and what we do as guided by the Holy Spirit. As an extension of this, Titus 3:2 tells us we should have humility in all we do. The absence of this pride also includes a mindset that says we are to make great efforts to do things for others without any expectation that we will yield any benefit from it. Nelson Henderson once profoundly said: "The true meaning of life is to plant trees, under whose shade you do not expect to sit."

We are not to just be a reservoir of spirituality as Christians, but also a fountain. By this I mean others should see and feel the excitement and aliveness we have from the joy of the Holy Spirit in us. This does not occur through rote memorizations of scripture and understanding doctrines or mechanical adherence to a set of rules and systems. It occurs through meeting people where they are and demonstrating love for them. When I was in 9th grade, I took a Latin class and studied very hard. The teacher was not concerned with how we used the language or its application but instead, was completely focused on rote and mechanical memorization. This is how he defined success, and I believe, how the school defined it as well. I got an 'A' in the class and on the last day, I was so upset as to the "how" and the method of the teacher's instruction (and the complete lack of how it fit into my life), that I tore up the entire textbook page by page and threw it out. So, although on the outside, I had proved that I had mastered the topic and, on the outside (on a scholastic level) my cup was clean - on the inside, there was no fountain around this subject, no motivation or vigor to remember the material, incorporate it into my life or continue with its study. The irony was that in later years, I began to really appreciate Latin and the fact that so many of our English words are taken from Latin (as well as other wonderful languages). As Christians, we need to create a fountain in others by them seeing it on our faces.

Aspect # 5

We are to live in the Spirit after we are saved along with living up to the amazing responsibility that comes with that freedom. Continually sinning after we are saved is inconsistent with our new nature in Christ. <u>Out of the love we constantly receive from God through the spiritual knowledge we have by having become born-again, we are more acutely aware of God's expectations of us using our gifts and talents to glorify Him through our genuine and complete love towards others.</u> The only way we have even the slightest chance of living a life free of sin (and holding to the Commandment of the New Covenant to able to fully love others) is if we have the Holy Spirit in us as born-again believers; and allow that Spirit to work through us unto these perfect works. Since the sin nature still resides in us after we become saved, there is still great temptation to view God's unconditional love for us as freedom to do whatever we want. This is a misuse in the trust God has for us and taking advantage of His love and grace. When someone trusts us with something and asks us to be responsible, our maturity and sense of accountability in us demands (and requires) we rise to the occasion, stand up and be counted, and demonstrate integrity which defines our character in that moment, even if no one is watching. As can be seen by how we act in each moment of our life, no one ever takes away our integrity; we only lose it if we give it away. With this, the following verses testify as to the importance of not using God's complete and total forgiveness of our sins as a free right to sin and abound in that sin:

- Galatians 5:13-14 – My brothers, we have all been called to freedom and liberty and we are not to use liberty for an occasion to the flesh, but by love serve one another. For all the law is fulfilled in one word, even in this; you should love your neighbor as yourself.

- I Peter 1:14-16 - As believers and children of God, we are not to shape ourselves according to the former lusts in our ignorance and sin nature: But as He which has called you us Holy, so we should be Holy in all manner of conversation; Because it is written, Be ye Holy; for I am Holy.

- I John 3:6,9 – Christians will sometimes inadvertently sin but they are not to make it a practice.

- II Corinthians 3:17 - …and where the Spirit of God is, there is also liberty.

- James 1:25 - But whoever looks into the perfect law of

liberty, and continues there, he being not a forgetful hearer, but a doer of the work, this man shall be blessed in his deed.

- Galatians 5:1 – It was for freedom that Christ set us free.

- A roman 8:2 – For the law of the Spirit of life in Christ Jesus has set you free.

- John 8:36 – If therefore the Son shall make you free, you shall be free indeed.

Sinning, and/or making sin a habit after we have become a believer, is inconsistent with our new nature and identity in Christ. This does not mean we will always act perfectly as believers but it does mean that sinful acts are out of line as to God's expectations for us and how we use the many individual and unique gifts He has given us. The following verses explain our nature and identity as a Christian along with the responsibility and personal accountability to live as such under its grace:

I Corinthians 6:17	You are one spirit with the Lord.
I Corinthians 12:27	You are a member of Christ's body.
Colossians 2:10	You are complete in Christ.
Philippians 1:6	You are confident that the good work God has begun in me will be perfected.
Philippians 3:20	You are a citizen of Heaven.
II Timothy 1:17	You have not been given a spirit of fear, but of power, love, and a sound mind.
Matthew 5:13-14	You are the salt and light of the earth.
Philippians 4:13	You can do all things through Christ who strengthens you.

With this in mind, it is difficult to imagine that as Christians, we would seek out opportunities to sin or to make sinning a habitual practice; especially after we have been trusted and accepted by God to walk in the newness of the resurrected life of His Son, guided by the Holy Spirit. God not only expects us to live up to the freedom He has given to us, but also trusts us fully (as His children) to take full spiritual responsibility in treating others to the same degree of unconditional love and acceptance that we ourselves believe God shows to us. To this extent, we are only able to love others on this earth to the same degree, depth and quality as compared to that which we believe is shown to us from God – no more and no less.

We are not to turn back once we have been given guidance by the Holy Spirit into areas of our lives (Luke 9:62) and the gifts given to us by God should not be neglected (I Timothy 4:14). We are to present our bodies as living sacrifices to God and honor Him in all that we do (Romans 12:1, I Corinthians 6:19) and are to have total confidence God will take care of our every need (I Timothy 1:5, Philippians 4:13) and will support us in accomplishing things that He has set out for us to do. We are to be a doer and demonstrate our love for others (James 1:22) and not just one who recites doctrines. Romans 10:9-13 tells us to be humble and meek. Titus warns us against engaging in senseless arguments with others as well. I Corinthians 9:19-21 instructs us to witness to others as to our first love as we experienced the saving grace of God through Christ and share His message so others may share in this great joy of eternal salvation. Indeed, with this freedom we have also comes tremendous responsibility.

Through the process of growing in grace, we slowly gain a greater and deeper understanding of what it is to love and shine the light God has given to us (I Corinthians 13 and Matthew 5) - not how we, from a carnal standpoint, define it. This process of growing in grace is one we allow to occur through opening ourselves up to the will of God and progressively turning over the control in our lives to the Holy Spirit in all things. It is human nature for us to resist this at every turn because of our need to control, our reliance on intellectual or human rationalizations for our actions, our false sense of security we find in the things of this world and our inability to trust and feel secure in God's will (priorities) and in His methods in how they are applied to our lives. As Paul states in Romans, we are constantly battling the 'old man' (sin nature) and, even when we try to do good and not sin, we fail. It is not we who have the capability to stop ourselves from sinning. Instead, it is us allowing the Holy Spirit to govern our lives so that we keep from sinning with His guidance. But even if we sin, it is great to know we have Christ as our intercessor and mediator maintaining our spiritual identity with God as spiritually perfect in His eyes, constantly and completely forgiven.

Going Beyond The Expectations Of The Old Covenant

Another extremely important aspect of living in the Spirit after we are saved and the responsibility that comes with that freedom is that we are to go beyond the expectations of that which was required from us under the Old Covenant Law. It is surprising to many Christians to fully realize the extent to which this should be true in our lives according to God's desire for us under grace. There are numerous examples in the Bible which demonstrate this truth and galvanize the fact that, under grace and the New Covenant, <u>God's expectations are much higher for us than that which was in the Old Covenant Law</u>. The table below outlines many of these verses. None of these expectations are listed in the Old Covenant Law, yet they are certainly standards which Jesus established as critical to living out the grace message. As you read, keep in mind that God rarely - if at all - ever challenged us in the Old Covenant to examine our heart since our relationship with God in that Covenant was based solely on our behavior and actions and not our intent or heart related issues which drove those behaviors. However, God does make this an integral part of our relationship with Him under the New Covenant:

Matthew 19:16-24	A man comes to Jesus and says he has kept the entire law and deserves to get into Heaven. Jesus challenges him to give away all his riches to the poor and the man is devastated.
Matthew 5:19-22	Jesus tells us that the Old Covenant Ten Commandments told us we should not kill, but the New Covenant under Grace tells us that even if we have anger in our hearts, we have committed murder.
Matthew 5:39-41	Instead of "an eye for an eye", we are told we should "turn the other cheek". Christ also tells us to walk an extra mile if one asks us to unfairly only walk one.
Matthew 5:43	We are not only to love our neighbor but are also to love our enemies.
Matthew 6:1-18	We are not to have the heart of a hypocrite.
Matthew 6:25-31	We are to have complete faith that God will always take care of our every need.
Matthew 18:23-33	God expects us to use our talents and blessings to the same degree that we are blessed.
Matthew 20:1-12	God loves pure intent and not necessarily outward action which many times doesn't represent what is truly in our hearts.
Mark 3:4-5	Jesus was healing someone on the Sabbath which was clearly against the Old Covenant law. The Pharisees used this as an example to malign Jesus and the Grace he advocated under the New Covenant.
Mark 7:8	Jesus scolds people who are holding onto the Old Covenant at the expense of embracing Grace.
Mark 10:19-25 & Luke 18:19-25	A man comes to Jesus and says he has kept the entire law and deserves to get into Heaven. Jesus challenges him to give away all his riches to the poor and the man is devastated.
Luke 14:12-14	Jesus tells the people that when they give a dinner, to not just invite the rich and famous who can pay you back and benefit you but invite the poor and those with disabilities who may not be able to repay you.

God challenges us to have a personal relationship with Jesus in the New Covenant. This relationship is personal because we may be asked by God and challenged to do things in our Christian walk that others may not; and vice versa. God has given each of us very special unique talents and gifts and, within that personal relationship we have, only God and each of us knows the extent to which those gifts are given as well as the unique and personal challenge we have from God. The versus above make the point that, under the New Covenant, the expectations God has for us go well beyond keeping the Ten Commandments and just being a "good" person in the eyes of others. Each one of us are given a special high standard and calling from God; and we will be held accountable as to how we use those gifts to glorify Him as we show love towards others.

In the field of education, there are two main methods to grade people. One is referred to as 'norm referenced instruction' and the other is 'criterion referenced instruction'. With norm referenced, everyone in the class is graded on a curve, normal distribution or averages where a certain percentage get an A, a certain percentage get a B and so on. In criterion referenced instruction, there is a specific and established criterion for what we need to achieve. It does not matter what others in the class do and the individual's grade or score will not be influenced, averaged or determined by what they do. It is between you and the criterion or objectively set standard. Our relationship with God is much like this. God gives us unique and special gifts and expects us to make our special contribution to this world based on those gifts. For those who have been blessed with much, God expects much. What we do in God's eyes based on these gifts is not graded on a "norm" or in comparison with others. God expects much more from us based on his objective "criterion" or standard of us. This standard is set differently for each person based on their gifts, talents, and convictions. To whom much is given, much is expected. It is different for each person. This is a significant part of what a personal relationship with the Lord means. It is a relationship based on grace which only we know all of the personal and intimate dynamics of.

To close this aspect, we are not to minimize the impact of the gifts and talents we are blessed with by adhering to rigid regulations of certain churches and having an outward appearance of wisdom, self-denial and false self-humility. This is the equivalent of cleaning the cup on the outside while it remains filthy dirty on the inside.

Aspect # 6

Closely linked to the previous aspect is the realization that we have a personal relationship with God and that, although there are many similarities in what our Christian walk's should look like as a body of believers, each individual Christian relationship with God is completely unique from another's. Hebrews 4:12 states: What God says to us is full of His living power and goes to our most intimate and personal thoughts and feelings. His Word exposes us for who we are as we relate to God through the reading and studying of it. We are to prepare ourselves to be objective and open to God's instruction in our lives and be willing to have a teachable spirit and humble ourselves to God and others (paraphrased). James 4:10-11 states that: "Humble yourselves in the sight of the Lord, and He will lift you up, and do not speak evil of one another..." II Peter 1:3-9 states we are given great and precious promises: that by these we might be partakers of the divine nature, having escaped the corruption that is in the world through lust. And beside this, through our perseverance, we add to our faith virtue; and to virtue knowledge; and to knowledge temperance; and to temperance patience; and to patience godliness; and to godliness brotherly kindness; and to brotherly kindness, charity. For if these things be in you, and abound, they make you that you should neither be barren nor unfruitful in the knowledge of our Lord Jesus Christ.

In Hebrews 13:1-2, the writer is making the point that we should always act and treat others as though we were in God's presence: Let brotherly love continue and don't be forgetful when you are in the company of strangers because the stranger you're with may just be an angel in your presence you are unaware of. With this personal relationship with God, we are to use our gifts and talents for His glory. We are uniquely challenged in ways that only each person is aware of. In many ways, it is a private and special agreement that God has with each one of us based on the special nature of each person's talents and gifts (Romans 12:6, I Corinthians 12, II Corinthians 8:12, I Corinthians 3:8-10 and Mark 10:44).

Aspect # 7

Discussed in a later chapter, our prayers have several key purposes:

- For us to accept, trust and believe in God's will for us which He has pre-ordained and is already aware of;

- For us to realize the full extent of God's grace and love that He has already given to us as a Christian;

- For us to individually be more convicted through meditation with His Holy Spirit which resides in us as to how we should love others.

- To help us to slow down our decision-making process and reflect on what God's word has to say about whatever is on our mind (whether it is a problem to be solved, an action we should take or a focus we should have).

As subscripts to these four areas, we can realize that:

- When we pray, the most important thing is to pray for God's will to be done – even if it is contrary to what our sin-nature and human desires really want.

- When we pray, we are demonstrating to ourselves and to others who may be listening that we are humbling ourselves before a sovereign God who loves us and will take care of our every need.

- If we believe we must pray to God for Him to provide our needs then we are simultaneously saying He will not meet our needs unless we are making our requests known to Him through prayer. This says that our prayers cause God to do something; which is untrue. This is a misguided idea of what our needs are because if we don't pray for them to be met, God will not grant them; and our needs will then not be met. Yet we know God takes care of all our needs – with or without us praying for them. This will be further discussed in the Chapter on prayer.

Aspect # 8

With great acceptance and peace, having a full understanding that blessings we receive from God not only take the form of things that immediately go right for us or make us happy in the moment but that also, we are fully blessed when things don't go the way we want; even when tremendous difficulties are present. We should have total confidence in God's love for us - resting in the fact that we have tremendous spiritual riches and security. But, we are also blessed when things don't go well in our lives. In these times of trouble, we can still benefit from opportunities and learn valuable lessons which we otherwise might not have learned. I Thessalonians 5:18 says that in all things we should give thanks because this is the will of God in Christ concerning us. In I Corinthians 2:9 Paul writes that God has many amazing blessings in store for all those who are believers. This is even true (and sometimes especially true) in times of difficulties.

Romans 5:3-5 says we should glory in difficulties also knowing that tribulations works patience; and patience, experience; experience, hope: and hope makes us not ashamed; because the love of God is shed abroad in our hearts by the Holy Spirit which is given to us. James 1:2-4 states: "My fellow brothers, count it all joy when ye fall into difficult temptations; knowing this, that the trying of your faith works patience." II Corinthians 12:10 continues with the same rationale: "Therefore I take pleasure in infirmities, in reproaches, in necessities, in persecutions, in distresses for Christ's sake: for when I am weak, then am I strong."

Conclusion

God makes us perfect in every good work to do His will, working in us that which is well pleasing in His sight, through Christ and guided by the Holy Spirit which indwells in each believer (Hebrews 13:21). Paul, in Galatians 3:1-3, teaches us that if we come to God through Christ and enter His Spirit our good deeds and works come from that Spirit and not from our carnal selves causing our salvation. He states: You foolish Galatians, who has told you untrue stories and tempted you with other gospel messages that are completely false, that you should not obey the truth, before whose eyes Jesus Christ hath been evidently set forth, crucified among you? Did you receive the Spirit of God by the works of the law and your good deeds, or by simply the hearing of faith and believing? Are you all so foolish? Having begun in the Spirit, are you now made perfect by the flesh? (paraphrased) The guiding light for the Christian is the Grace of God as given to us by the Holy Spirit.

Christians are constantly trying to change their lives and make marginal alterations to their existing person, but God calls us to experience an entire new identity. He doesn't want us to perfect the old nature (or our old foundation). He wants us to have a new nature and identity in Him through Christ. Sometimes we are too conditioned to our old life and this prevents us from moving forward. As Christians, we sometimes refuse the new life Christ has in store for us. We are so used to doing things our way through habit, tradition, or misplaced spiritual beliefs, that when a better way comes along (God's plan of salvation and living in grace resting from all of our actions to prove ourselves worthy) we are reluctant and unwilling to yield ourselves to it.

It is only in comparison to the riches of knowing Christ that sin begins to lose its appeal. The leadership guru Stephen Covey (as it relates to leadership and priority management) refers to this as the "bigger yes". There are many things in our lives which we can choose and say "yes" to but in doing so, other things get put to the side and become secondary. Each of us must ask ourselves what the biggest things in our lives are that we should say yes to. If we are in Christ, we are in the light. Many scriptural verses tell us that when we sin in the light it is more difficult and not as enjoyable. If we are born-again believers, we have Christ in us and therefore when we sin, we must sin in the light. God's blessing continues to be with us as believers, however. As we enter into sin, God has already forgiven us, and with that forgiveness, comes Grace and blessings in our lives. Its just that, through this sin that God does not intend for us, we are not as able to realize and experience His full blessing in our lives.

Through the process of growing in grace, we slowly gain a greater and deeper understanding of what it is to love and shine the light that God has given to us (as is described in I Corinthians 13 and Matthew 5) - not how we, from a carnal standpoint, define it. This process of growing in grace is one that we allow to occur through opening ourselves up to the Will of God and turning over the control in our lives to the Holy Spirit in all things. It is human nature for us to resist this at every turn because of our need to control, our reliance on intellectual or human rationalizations for our own actions, and our inability to trust and feel secure in God's priorities and in His methods. As Paul states in Romans, we are constantly battling the 'old man' and, even when we try to do good and not sin, we fail. It is not we who have the capability to stop ourselves from sinning. Instead, it is us allowing the Holy Spirit to govern our lives so that we keep from sinning with His guidance and direction. But even if we sin, it is great to know that we have Christ as our intercessor and meditator maintaining our spiritual identity with God as spiritually perfect in His eyes, constantly and completely forgiven.

The following passages help us understand the responsibility and opportunity for joy each born again believer has under grace:

- II Corinthians 5:17 states that if any person be in Christ, he/she is a new creature and that all our old things pass away in God's time and therefore, all things become new.
- Philippians 1:6 states that we should be confident of this very thing, that he who has begun a good work in each Christian will perform it until the day Christ returns.
- II Corinthians 9:8 tells us that God's grace abounds and multiplies to meet every need the Christian has.
- I Corinthians 3:10 states that God's grace has empowered us to do all service for others in love according to the gifts and blessings he has given to each Christian.
- I Peter 5:5 states that God gives grace to those who are humble.
- Finally, I Corinthians 15:10 and II Corinthians 12:9 tell us that we have sufficiency in God's grace for all things in this world.

Reflection & Study Questions For This Chapter:

- Forgiveness by God, through Christ, is only half of the message of salvation. The other half is accepting and living in Christ's resurrected life with the Holy Spirit inside us. The word "hope" is never used in the Old Testament but it is used over 75 times in the New Testament. Why is this important, and how does it apply to our everyday lives?
- What does I Corinthians 1:19-2:16 mean to you and how do you think it applies, or could apply to your life?
- If I John 1:9 was written to unbelievers, and not believers, what are the ramifications for us?
- Do you believe that every time you sin you need to: Ask God for forgiveness? Ask the person(s) you offended for forgiveness? Or both? Why?
- Which verse(s) in the Bible testify as to the importance of not using God's complete and total forgiveness of our sins as a free right to sin and abound in that sin?
- Do you believe the blessings we receive from God only take the form of things that go right for us or make us happy in the moment? Or do you believe God blesses us when things don't go well, even when tremendous difficulties are present? Can you think of a time in your life where things did not go well but you knew God was still with you and blessing you?

Chapter 5

Death Of Our Human Desires and Sin Nature

Romans 5:12-19 says that by one man's disobedience (Adam), we were born with a sin nature and therefore, we are all made sinners. These versus also say there is another law (the sin nature) in our members other than our spiritual nature, even after we become saved. The process of growing in grace involves the Holy Spirit working through us to overcome the overwhelming desires in our sin nature and help us to grow spiritually becoming progressively sanctified on this earth; or at least as sanctified as is possible according to each person's unique set of circumstances, challenges, gifts, blessings, and choices. Sanctification refers to the ongoing progress the Holy Spirit makes in our lives as to how we can grow in grace and demonstrate love towards others. Romans 5:3,4 tells us tribulations in our lives produce perseverance, that perseverance produces character and character results in hope (the path the sin nature goes through in being overcome by the power of the Holy Spirit in each believer).

The journey of the sin nature in becoming absorbed by the Spirit nature inside us is a long one filled with much resistance; involving choices that all too often take us away from God's best will for us. However, as Christians it is our challenge to be accountable and make the best choices that reflect the leading of the Holy Spirit through our life and daily activities. Through this, we can step outside ourselves (figuratively) and watch as the sin nature dies in this moment by moment, daily, monthly, yearly and lifelong process as is summarized in the following versus:

Galatians 2:20	We have been crucified with Christ, and it is no longer I who live but Christ who lives in me (in the form of the Holy Spirit). Paul continues by saying

	that "the life which I live now in the flesh I live by faith in the Son of God".
Romans 6:16-19	What we present ourselves slaves to we will obey; whether it is giving into the sin-nature or following the leading of the Holy Spirit. We are to make the choice to present ourselves followers of our new nature.
Romans 6:3-12	When we took Christ as our savior, we were baptized in His death and we are to walk in the newness of life. Our old sin-nature is united with His death and our new spiritual nature is united with His resurrection in newness of life. Our "old man" (old sin-nature) was crucified with Him in that the body of sin may be done away with and we would no longer be slaves of sin but be able to choose righteous thoughts and actions over the fruits of the sin-nature. We are to reckon ourselves to be dead to sin by employing (allowing) the Holy Spirit to drive our urges and desires.
I Peter 4:1	Since Christ suffered for us in the flesh, we are to have the same mind and let our fleshly desires suffer and not give it what it wants; essentially with the goal of ceasing from sin.
Philippians 1:21-23	To allow my sin nature to die is gain but if I live on in the flesh and give in to its evil desires and wants, I will not be in control of my choices and I will choose things that may not be consistent with my new nature. I struggle with this paradox: to depart from Christ and give into my desires or think and do that which is in Christ.
Philippians 3:8	Paul counts all of the loses he experiences (that the sin nature does not get) as excellence in terms of increasing his knowledge of Christ and growing in his relationships with Him. The things he has lost, that the sin nature really wanted and desired, he counts them as garbage in comparison with the

	gain he receives in following the new nature (Holy Spirit).
II Corinthians 4:6-12	As believers, God has commanded light to shine out of darkness but the sin nature inside of us believes we have certain treasures here on earth and therefore wants to hold onto them. These earthly temptations, which appeal to the sin nature, are all around us, but we should not be in despair, feel struck down or forsaken. We are to focus on the life of Christ being in us (in our mortal flesh) so that death is working in us (as we deny the sin nature what it wants) while life is working in us with Christ through the Holy Spirit.
I John 2:16	All that is in the world (the lust of the flesh, lust of the eyes, and the pride of life), is not of the father but is of the world.
I Peter 2:9-11	We have been called out of darkness and are people of God and are to abstain from fleshly lusts which war against our souls.
I Peter 4:2,3	As Christians, we are to no longer live our lives in the flesh for the lusts of men but instead for the will of God. We have spent enough time in our past doing the will of the flesh when we walked in lewdness, lusts, revelries and abominable idolatries.
Romans 8:2	The law of the Spirit of life in Christ has made me free from the law of sin and death.
Romans 8:10,13	Since Christ is in us, the body is dead because of sin but the Spirit is life because of righteousness. When we live by the Spirit, we put to death the deeds of the body.
Romans 13:13,14	We are to make no provision for the flesh to fulfill its lusts. We are supposed to walk properly according to the Spirit not in lust, lewdness, envy and strife.
Colossians 3:5	We are to put to death our members which are on the earth and which are contrary to the Spirit (evil,

	covetousness, idolatry and uncleanness).
Galatians 5: 16,17	We are to live by the Spirit and not give into the sin nature. The flesh lusts against the Holy Spirit and the Spirit against the flesh and these are contrary to one another – so you do not do the things you wish.
I Corinthians 15:31	Since I have Christ in me, I die daily in this world. In other words, the desires of my once dominating sin nature dies daily as it repeatedly does not get what it desires.
Romans 8:3-9	God condemned sin in the flesh when He sent Christ to us and once we are in Christ, we are to walk according to the Spirit and not the flesh. The carnal mind is at enmity and complete disagreement to God's will and his Spirit. As Christians, we are not in the flesh but in the Spirit.
John 3:30	Christ must increase in me and I (what I want based in my sin nature) must decrease.

As we go through this process of growing in grace, and our sin nature diminishes inside each of us as it is dominated by the Holy Spirit, we go through a process of saying goodbye to the past and to that sin nature that once dominated everything we did. For the carnal self, this is an extremely painful process accompanied by tremendous emotional baggage and casualties attached; especially in terms of things we previously relied upon in this world to "get us through", provide security and help us cope. Basically, these are worldly reactions from our sin nature that helped us to survive and be effective in the carnal world. <u>The things we say goodbye to in this lifelong process are often those things which worked hard to prevent us in the first place from realizing we were born with a sin nature and giving our heart over to Jesus.</u> In short, this relates to an over reliance on this world along with an over reliance of its empty promises and surface level attractions. After we become born again, our sin nature becomes the lower less dominate nature; but it is still there. In essence, the process of growing in grace in our Christian life consists of us, with the direction of the Holy Spirit, being able to suppress the desires of the sin nature and prevent it from getting what it wants while simultaneously developing and growing the spiritual nature we are given at the time of our salvation. It involves letting go of the things that sin nature held onto so closely.

In the plains of Africa, monkeys can easily be trapped by putting nuts in containers attached to a rope. The monkeys put their hands in the mouth of the jars and grab the nuts which are inside. With their fists clenched, they are then unable to get their hands out of the jar. The trappers simply reel in the jar with the rope and grab the monkeys. If they were to just let go of the nuts and unclench their fists, they could take their hands out of the jar and easily escape; but they do not. This is a picture of what we do with the things of our sin nature in our spiritual life. If we would just release those things from our hands, our head and our hearts, we could then get away from the "jar" that keeps us trapped and pre-occupied in our sin natures and not focused as we should be on the things of the Spirit.

Reflection & Study Questions For This Chapter:

- If you do not know the Lord as your personal Savior, what things of, and in this world, are you holding onto which may be preventing you from making this choice?

- If you are saved and know the Lord, what things were holding you back - prior to your salvation - in making the commitment you made?

Chapter 6

The Spiritual Nature And Grief

Romans 6 tells us that after we have accepted Christ as our Savior, the part of us that loves to sin is crushed, shattered and "fatally wounded". The ultimate irresistible power over us is gone and sin is no longer our master. We can choose our master. The sin loving physical body and flesh is no longer under the complete control of the sin nature; it can freely choose the things of the Spirit. At the time of our salvation, the old sin nature is said to be buried and likened with the death and burial of Christ. We then share a new nature and a new life with the Holy Spirit indwelt in us. Sinning is inconsistent with our new nature. We understand however, that with this new nature as Christians, the old sin nature still resides in us and will until we die physically.

Romans 6:18 states that with our new spiritual nature, we have been set free from sin and have become slaves of righteousness. This means we are now fully aware of what is required of us according to the priorities of the Spirit and we are not free to "choose ignorance" or to go back to being unaware. To go back to acting as though we are unaware is the same as lying to ourselves. Romans 6:19 continues by saying we are to present our physical members as slaves of righteousness separate from the worldly desires. We are given a more complete burden of accountability to monitor, manage and control our physical members.

The following verses describe the dynamics (and often times battle) of the relationship between the sin nature and the spirit nature after the amazing event of becoming saved. The dynamics and principles outlined in these verses exist throughout our entire Christian walk until the day we physically die:

Romans 6:13	We are not to present our bodies as instruments of un-Godly things that follow the sin nature but instead, present ourselves to God as being alive from the dead and use our bodies for Godly things.
Romans 7:23-25	We have another law (the law of the sin nature and its carnal desires) that is at war with our Spiritual nature. When we follow that other law, we become captive to it and it 'becomes' us. Paul encourages us to make choices to follow the spiritual law in us and not the law of flesh and sin.
II Corinthians 4:6-12	God encourages us to have our light shine instead of our darkness but he knows we have our spiritual nature that is trapped inside our earthly shells; our physical bodies. Even though we are hard pressed, there is still His hope in us. Our sin nature was likened to Christ and His death at the Cross in that it no longer has complete dominion over us. We can freely choose to not follow and give into the desires and temptations the world puts in front of our sin nature.
Philippians 3:8	As I look at all the things I have lost each day, I see this as part of our road to spiritual excellence since the things I have lost are only desires of the sin nature which are garbage compared to the blessings I receive in living according to our spiritual nature.
Galatians 5:17	The sin nature desires that which is opposite of the Spirit and the Spirit against the flesh. They are each contrary to each other. Sometimes, the sin nature wins and we do not do the things that our Spiritual nature wants us to do.
I Thessalonians 4:4,5	Paul encourages us to be in control of our own vessels (physical bodies and sin nature) in sanctification and honor to God. We are to be in control so we do not follow the lusts of the flesh.

Matthew 5:6	Blessed are those who hunger and thirst for righteousness for they shall be filled. In this context, our spirit nature hungers and thirsts for the things of the spirit as the sin nature desires that which is temporary and of the world.
Mathew 6:26	Look at the birds of the air, for they neither sow nor reap nor gather in barns; yet God feeds them. We are more valuable to God than these birds and he will take care of our every need. God encourages us that our spiritual nature defines our true needs and our sin nature defines our wants, which are not aligned with the things of our spiritual nature.
Matthew 6:24	No man can serve two masters; for either he will hate the one and love the other or else he will be loyal to the one and desire the other. We cannot serve God and mammon (things of the sin nature) both.
Matthew 16:24	Jesus tells His disciples that if anyone desires to follow Him, that he should deny himself and take up the Cross (of living in this world with a sin nature) and follow Christ.
Luke 9:23	Luke's account of this same phrase emphasizes the importance for us to take up our Cross daily. He is referring to the challenge we have as Christians daily to meet the difficulties of following the Spiritual nature while the sin nature and fleshly desires fights against us.
I John 4:2,4,13	We can have confidence that we are able to abide in God and live according to His will for us since we have been given His Spirit. We should be extremely careful to test whether things are coming from the Spiritual nature or the sin nature in this world. We can be comforted in knowing that we can overcome what is in this world since he who is in us is greater than that which is of this world.

I Peter 2:11	Peter encourages us to be sojourners and pilgrims and make choices to not follow the lusts of the flesh and the sin nature which are constantly fighting against us.
II Peter 2:10	Peter encourages us not to walk according to the lusts of the flesh and uncleanness. Those who follow the desires of the sin nature are presumptuous and self willed.
Titus 2:12	God tells us to deny ungodliness and worldly lusts.

As we go through the process of growing in grace, our Spiritual nature is supposed to dominate our lives more and more, not only compared to what we allow in the things of the sin nature, but more importantly, according to God's absolute expectation of us. We become more mature as Christians and are better able to allow the Holy Spirit to dominate our lives unencumbered by our own personal and earthly carnal agendas. This is the essence of us "eating the meat" of God's Word as it applies to our life and no longer just "drinking the milk of His Word". As we mature spiritually, we are to challenge ourselves to live into our potential as defined by the leading of God as guided by the Holy Spirit. Day by day, month by month, and year by year, our sin nature begins to die in more parts of our lives and the spiritual nature dominates proportionately. As this occurs, the sin nature (dominated by our human and carnal desires and what we have come to know and trust in this world) goes through a process of significant change and grieving the loss of what it wanted; wants based on its self-centeredness, carnal desires, pride, world views, and what it has relied on in this world as security and essentially, all the things of the sin nature.

Elizabeth Kublais-Ross wrote a book in 1969 called "On Death and Dying". In it, she outlined the five "Stages of Grief" that people go through when they are facing the reality they are going to die or experience a tremendous loss. Most of her work dealt with those who were near death due to cancer. Her research also showed that people went through these stages of grief when confronted with the death of a loved one or if they had experienced a major traumatic event in their life that involved great loss or significant trauma. As can be seen in the picture below, these stages begin with shock and denial where we say things like: "There's no way this is true and it just can't be". The next stage is a flood of emotions (usually anger) where we become emotionally overwhelmed and get extremely upset that a particular occurrence may be coming true (or is true). The third stage is bargaining where we try to marginalize things or just let a little bit of that truth into our awareness because letting it all in is just too painful. Bargaining involves keeping some of the old while introducing just a little of the new. It involves marginalizing the impact of the event by accepting some of it onto our consciousness. The next stage is depression where we begin to understand and accept that what we fear is going to happen (or has happened) regardless of anything we do, we are upset with it and must accept the reality, but since it is very upsetting to us and there is not much we can do, we become depressed. Eventually, this leads to us accepting it. Acceptance has two phases however: first is intellectual acceptance where we accept it with our "head" in the context of compliance and intellectually getting our heads around it. The second part or phase is emotional acceptance where we can not only internalize the event but are able to accept it in its true reality and possibly, proactively and energetically look for any opportunities and blessings in the event through this full acceptance of it.

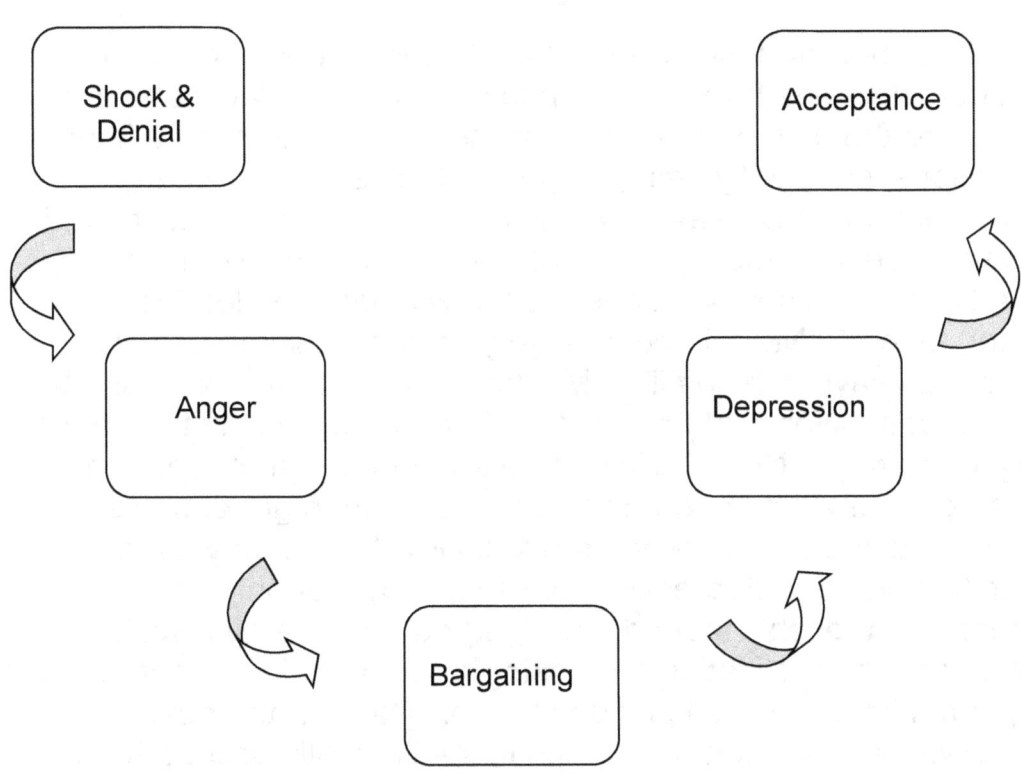

Through the process of growing in grace, and the sin nature not getting what it wants on a daily basis (or as often as it desires), our sin nature, and the desires stemming from the flesh, goes through the grief process very similar to the stages of grief outlined by Kublais-Ross in her book. As Christians living our lives and making choices which reflect our spiritual nature, but still having carnal desires inside of us, we experience many events or situations where we do not receive what our sin nature wants and desires. In these circumstances, our sin nature (and that part of us that chooses to allow the sin nature to maintain its hold on us) goes through these stages of grief.

An example may help to understand this. If I have been praying about that great job I've wanted for the last year and I find out that I didn't get it, initially I may react with shock and denial by saying that "I can't believe I didn't get the job". It is so upsetting to me that I deny that it is true. Once I begin to get more facts about it and realize that I, in fact, did not get the job, I experience a flood of emotions; especially being angry, and possible extreme disappointment. My heart, my actions and my words reflect that I am very upset and disappointed about this. I may even be angry at God about this saying things like "How could God let this happen to me"? Next, I begin to bargain and let some of this reality in by saying things like "Maybe there is another similar job at that organization that I can get" or "it probably wasn't that great of a job anyway". Next, I allow more and more of that reality in and, through my increased awareness; I begin to get depressed. It is now hitting me at a deep emotional level and I may even soften this hurt and depression by saying "I'm not only not interested in the job" (that I did not get) but my energy level is drained and my motivation for looking for another job is lost. I adopt an attitude where I just don't care. Through the next several weeks and months, I begin to intellectually accept the situation by logically looking around for other employment (although my heart is really not in it all the way and I am still upset and depressed about the job I didn't get). Finally, I begin to emotionally accept the situation, trying to accept this as being part of God's perfect will and then try to look for any opportunities or hidden blessings or lessons there may be in this situation.

As we go through our lives, day by day and year by year, we experience multiple events and circumstances which challenge the desires of our sin nature; just like the one described here. Continually and progressively, our sin nature goes through repeated instances or events where it's carnal desires are not realized and that part of us must accept it will not get what it wants; similar to a child not getting what they want. Through this process, the best result is that the sin nature diminishes through time and the spiritual nature dominates more and more in our lives as is represented by the picture. It should be clearly understood here that there are many examples of us going through the grief process which is completely consistent with God's word and is completely natural, necessary and healthy as part of God's plan and how He created us. For example, when a loved one dies. Aside from these moments, what I am referring to here is not the normal psychological grief process that God has made inside us that is necessary and beautiful. I am referring to the grief process of our sin nature; that part of us that is inconsistent with God's perfect plan for each of us and that part of us that wants to hold onto those aspects of the sin nature which used to comfort us, provide security for us and provide fun and excitement to us. Through this, it is very important to realize that all change produces fear and all change produces loss. It is fascinating to think about how the sin nature and the spiritual nature each process these two dynamics. Certainly, where change is put into our lives by God, the spiritual nature has no fear in the change, and the spiritual nature interprets the loss as an opportunity for us to grow in our Christian walk.

Our sin nature never completely dies and goes away. Even as mature Christians, at times these desires from the sin nature re-enter our lives possibly even stronger than before as Satan continues to tempt us and interfere with our Christian walk. It will always be there in us (to some degree) until the day God takes us home to Heaven. Throughout our lives, we may sin but we are not to let sin reign in our mortal bodies and continually obey its lusts. We are not to continue to present the members of our body as instruments of unrighteousness (Romans 6).

An important point in these five stages of grief is that this describes the process that the carnal sin nature goes through when it does not get what it wants in this world. The spiritual nature however, does not respond this way. It responds by examining what God is trying to teach us in the situation asking where is the blessing, what is His will and where is the opportunity for growth? It then moves quickly to acceptance of His will and a desire to take action that reflects the fruits of the Spirit and the characteristics of selfless love. God is the greatest cognitive therapist in that He encourages us to think with our minds, take action and then later let our emotions follow according to that which we can know from God's word. Proof of this is that He tells us in His Word that we may <u>know</u> we have eternal salvation; not that we may <u>feel</u> like we have it. As we progress in the process of Christian sanctification, the main goal with the sin nature going through the grief process is that it does not take as long and/or we do not go as deep in allowing this grief process to take hold in our hearts.

As an overlay to the above model which outlines the 5 primary stages of grief, I've added in the fruits of the Spirit in the diagram below along with principles of love found in I Corinthians. I've placed this on one end of the grief process which reflects God's desired outcome for us. On the other side, (where giving up aspects of the sin nature starts), I've placed the fruits of the sin nature. This way, we can get a better picture as to what the areas of our sin nature are that may have to go through the stages of grief as we make spiritual choices in our lives which prevent the sin nature from getting what it wants.

Fruits of Sin Nature (Galatians 5 and 6 & Romans 1:29)	Fruits of the Spirit (Galatians 5 & 6):
<ul><li>Adultery</li><li>Fornication</li><li>Sexual immorality</li><li>Uncleanliness</li><li>Lewdness</li><li>Idolatry</li><li>Sorcery</li><li>Hatred</li><li>Contentions</li><li>Jealousness</li><li>Covetousness</li><li>Wrath</li><li>Deceit</li><li>Selfish ambitions</li><li>Dissensions</li><li>Heresies</li><li>Envy</li><li>Murders</li><li>Violence</li><li>Drunkenness</li><li>Revelries</li><li>Pride</li><li>Keeping track of others faults</li><li>Conceited</li><li>Provoking</li><li>Wickedness</li><li>Maliciousness</li><li>Unforgiving</li><li>Untrustworthy</li></ul>	<ul><li>Love</li><li>Joy</li><li>Peace</li><li>Longsuffering</li><li>Kindness</li><li>Goodness</li><li>Faithfulness</li><li>Gentleness</li><li>Self control</li><li>Filled with humility</li><li>Unconditional love for others</li><li>Forgiveness</li><li>Perseverance</li><li>Patience</li></ul>

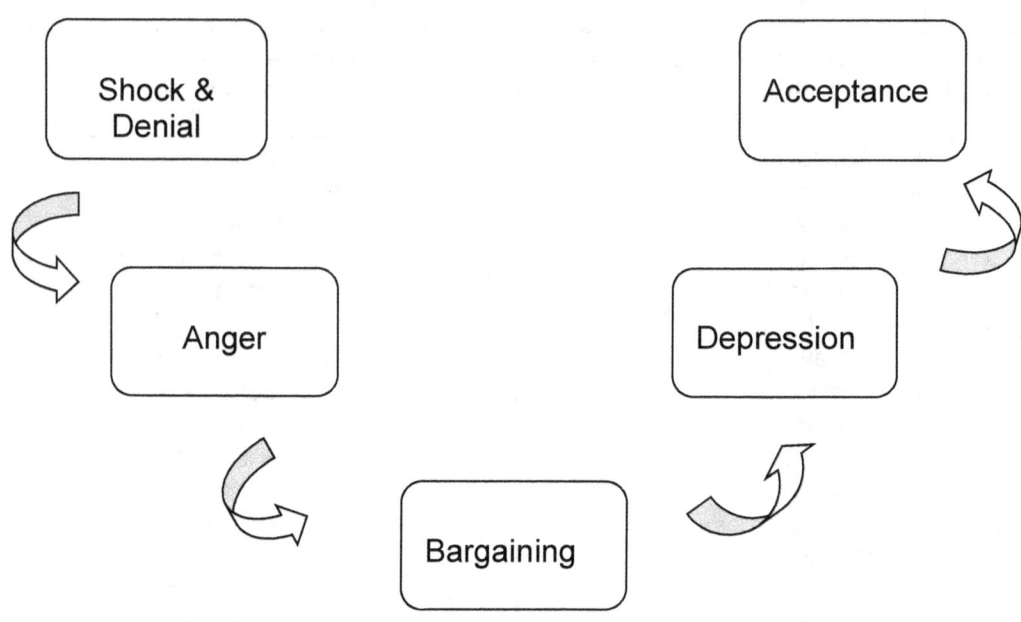

From the diagram above, the fruits of the sin nature are basically the desires of the flesh. As we go through our Christian walk and grow in grace, the desires of the sin nature (along with its wants) die a little each day; in fact numerous times each day. As we successfully go through the process of growing in grace with the guidance of the Holy Spirit, we are more able to demonstrate the fruits of the Spirit as we deny the things of the sin nature. To relate this grief process to our own lives, all we have to do is choose one of the bullets listed under the "Fruits of the Sin Nature" and think of an example in our life that we are convicted to give up (or have given up). For example, we can all think of something in our lives where we were or are being idolatrous such as worshiping money (or what it can buy), power, prestige, etc. As we grow in grace, and move away from this idolatrous behavior, a part of us (our sin nature) goes through the grief process. It first goes through shock and denial, then anger, then it bargains, then gets depressed and then eventually (as it moves towards the fruits of the spiritual nature), it begins to accept that this worship of money (or other sin) is wrong and is inconsistent with the things of the spiritual nature. The diagram below outlines our human state on one end of a time continuum throughout our life with attributes which are more consistent with God's intention for us.

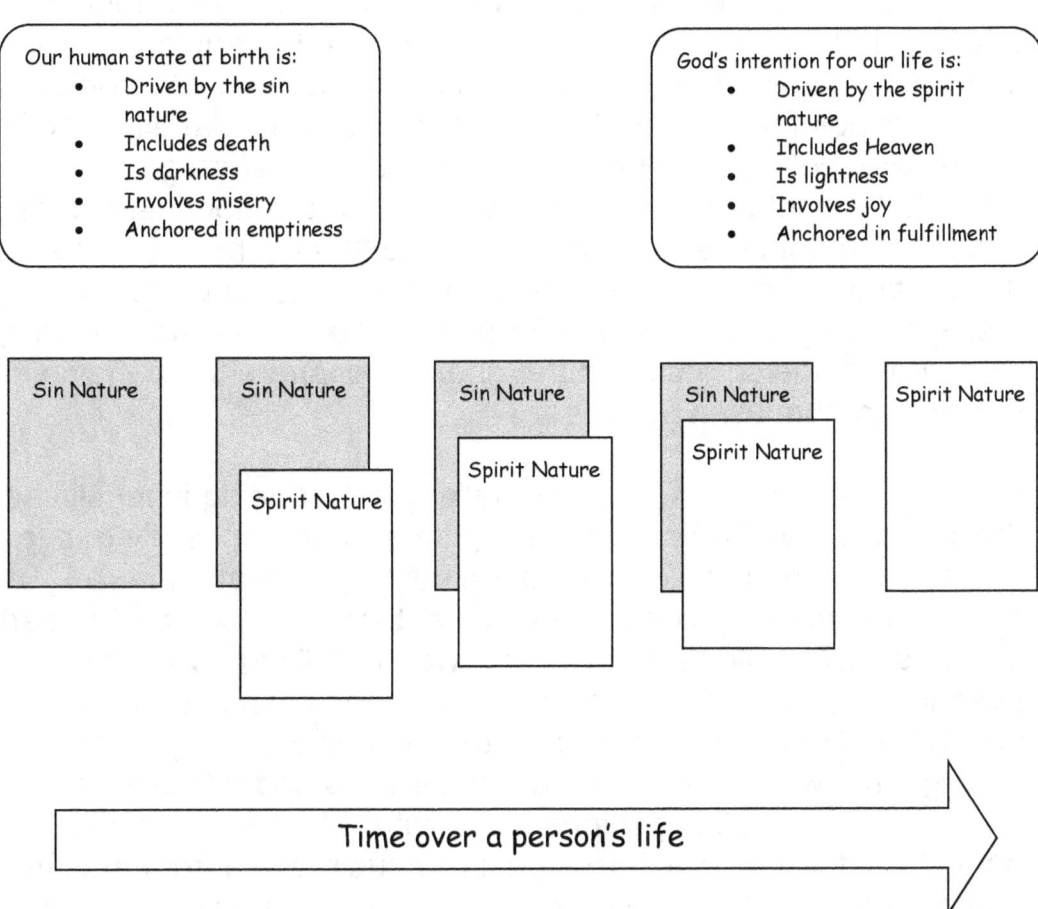

Through the stages of grief, and as we go through change in our lives, it is critical we understand that all loss (and change) produces fear. <u>As the sin nature deals with the loss it experiences each day as the Spiritual nature dominates more and more, tremendous fear is realized within our sin nature. The fear that the sin nature is experiencing relates to giving up trust in its</u>

111

<u>reliance on things of the world and the false security it has offered and the dependence the sin nature has on these things of the world.</u> As Christians, we have assurance from God that we can manage and deal with that fear in such a way that we are still effective. I John 4:17,18 says that perfect love has no fear and that perfect love casts out all fears. II Timothy 1:7 and Hebrews 13:6 tells us that the Holy Spirit inside us is more powerful than anything in the world. So, we should be able to handle any fear that these stages of grief produce in our sin nature. One other important point relating to these stages of grief is that all of the stages are feelings; not behaviors. As our sin nature goes through the grief process (as the spiritual nature dominates more and more in our lives), we can recognize that all these feelings are natural and normal to our old sin nature, but they are only feelings. They are no excuse for us to not grow in grace, develop the things of the spiritual nature, and demonstrate the behaviors God wants from us in our lives.

As mentioned above, we are not talking about being insensitive to the loss of a loved one or not taking time to appropriately grieve when an extremely difficult situation comes our way that challenges the things of our spiritual nature (and for which is part of God's perfect plan for us). What we are talking about is that, relating to the desires of the sin nature (those things that are contrary to God's perfect will for us), these stages of grief are feelings that we cannot allow to dominate us and prevent us from moving on and realizing things in our future that are within God's perfect will for us.   A different picture of us moving from the sin nature to the spiritual nature in our lives as each day passes by is depicted below. Our "whole person" is made up of part sin nature and part spiritual nature. As we grow in grace, we choose to what degree we are willing to allow the Holy Spirit to dominate in our lives so that we are primarily driven by the Holy Spirit who dwells in us. As the days pass by, the part of us that is the Spirit nature gets bigger and bigger until (hopefully) there is very little of the sin nature left in our lives. This all involves conscious choices we make in our lives.

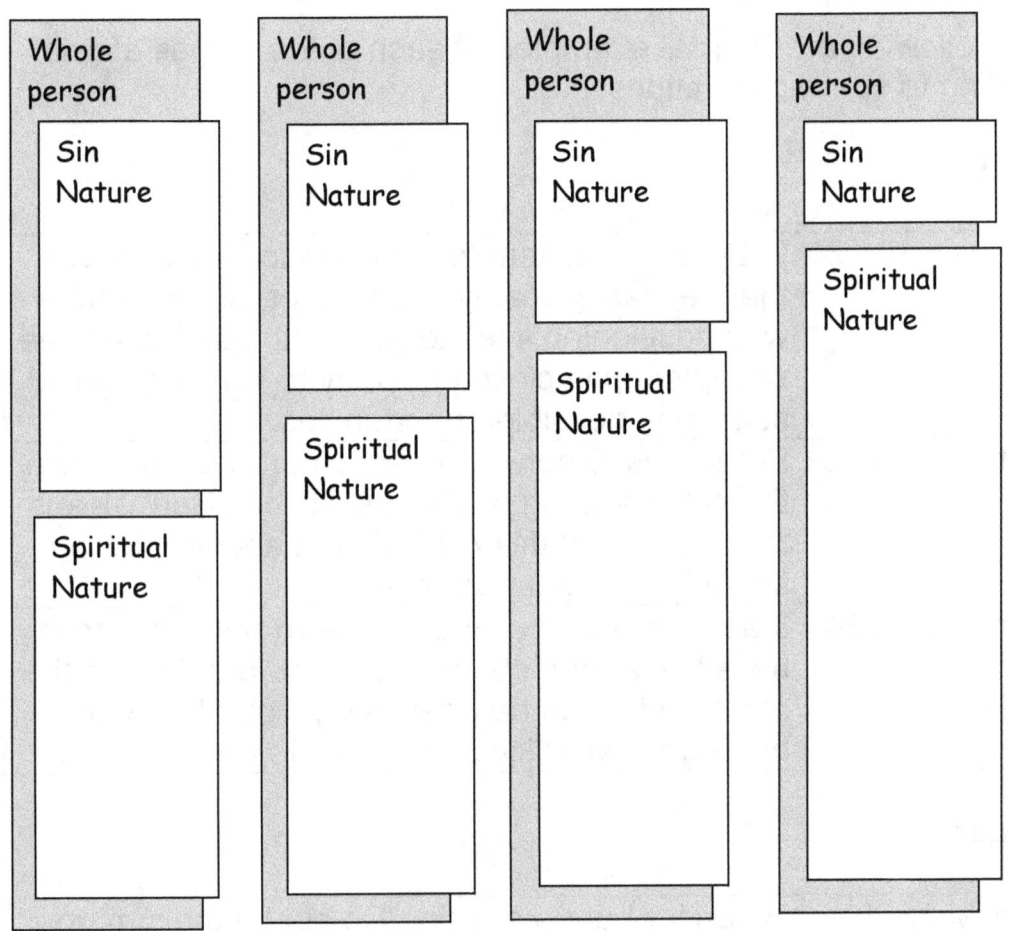

When we go through any type of change, there is fear involved and this fear is based on many questions we ask either consciously or unconsciously. Questions like: "Where will I end up after the change? What kind of losses will I have after the change? Will I be OK and will I be able to adjust to the new way?" God assures us that the answer to all these is "yes". One of the biggest comments Jesus made while he walked on this earth was that we should not have fear. This guidance is wonderful and directly applies to the struggle each of us goes through as Christians as we choose to give up more and more of the drives and actions of our sin nature.

The following are Biblical examples of each of the stages of grief relating to specific situations:

Denial

Genesis 13:12	Lot pitches his tent towards Sodom. At a level that he was probably unaware of, his sin nature was positioning itself to get what it desired as he set up shop in close proximity to sin so he could seize any possible opportunities.
Matthew 16:23	Peter tries to convince Jesus not to go into town the next morning or else he will be killed. Jesus tells Peter that this is God's will and that Satan should come out from him.
James 1:23,24	If anyone is a hearer of the word but not a doer, he is like a man observing his natural face in the mirror but when he goes away from the mirror, he forgets what kind of a man he was.

Anger

Ephesians 4: 26,31	Be angry but do not sin. Do not let the sun go down on your wrath. Let all bitterness, wrath, anger and evil speaking be put away from you. (Anger is a feeling, rage and inappropriate things we do are actions. They are separate.)
Ecclesiastes 7: 9	Do not hasten in your spirit to be angry because anger only rests in the hearts of fools.
James 1: 19-27 & Colossians 3:8	We are to be slow to wrath because the wrath of man does not produce the righteousness of God. Therefore, lay aside all evil wickedness and conduct yourselves with meekness.

Bargaining

Matthew 6:24	No man can serve two masters because he will hate the one and love the other or else he will be loyal to the one and despise the other. You cannot serve God and the sin nature.
Mathew 9:16,17	No one puts a piece of unshrunk cloth on an old garment because the patch will pull away from the garment and the hole will be worse.
Thematic through the Bible.	Moral relativism and situational ethics (altering the truth)
Thematic through the Bible.	Doing things that people find out about and saying "If others don't know about it it's OK.
Thematic through the Bible.	Comparing what you do with the actions of others which somehow make your actions comparative and not criterion based on your calling. This also means that you are not living and acting according to God's gifts to you or His unique expectations for your life.
Thematic through the Bible.	Incorrectly thinking that my goods outweigh my bads and therefore, a particular action is OK or at least that I can get by with doing it to some degree.

Depression (Grief)

I Thessalonians 4:13	We are not to become weary as we encounter difficulties but we are to maintain hope from God.
Mathew 5:4	Blessed are those who mourn for they shall be comforted.
John 16:20-22	Jesus tells us to have complete confidence that our sorrow will be turned into joy.

Acceptance

Matthew 13:44	Joy, from our own discovery of God, motivates us to sacrifice and serve and therefore experience tremendous blessings through the Holy Spirit.
I Timothy 6: 17 & Proverbs 15: 13	The joy we experience through appreciating God's gifts to us helps us to smile, sing and celebrate. We realize that we can have sadness and joy at the same time.
Mathew 8: 21-22	One of the disciples wanted to go and bury his father and Jesus said: let the dead bury their own dead.
II Corinthians 12:9	God assures us that His grace is sufficient for each of us and that our strengths are made perfect through our weaknesses.
I Peter 1: 6-7 & James 1:2	We have been grieved by various trials but getting through them has enabled us to experience thankfulness and blessings from God.
Philippians 4:11	Paul tells us to be accepting and happy no matter what state we are in.
Romans 5:3-4	God tells us that tribulations produce perseverance which produces character which produces hope.
Job 2:10	We should rejoice and accept it when we receive bad things in our life as well as good things.

Reflection & Study Questions For This Chapter:

- Are there areas of your life that your sin nature is holding onto, preventing you from moving forward spiritually? Where are you in the grief process in each of these areas?

- How can you move through the grief process and embrace more things of the spiritual nature as you grow in the Lord?

Chapter 7

Prayer

Prayer is talking to God in conversation. As Christians indwelt with the Holy Spirit, every moment of our lives is spent in 'conversation' with God as an ongoing, never ceasing dialogue. This is true whether our conversation takes the form of listening to Him, thanking Him for blessings given to us, meditating with Him, being in agreement with Him by being honest about our sins and mistakes, appreciating the wonder of His creation and/or demonstrating His will by showing unconditional love towards others. This means we are in prayer to God (or in conversation with Him) even when we don't have hands folded, eyes closed, knees bent and heads bowed.

Having this kind of mindset compels us to fully realize that God's Holy Spirit lives inside each of us at all times, as well as the spiritual responsibility and awesome privilege we enjoy living in the New Covenant where we are entitled to constantly be in His presence. Without having to go through a worldly mediator such as a priest or preacher, our relationship with God is not encumbered by a veil of separation or by the physical limitations of what this world requires of us through its standards and what it believes being a Christian consists of. Instead, we are (or should be) in a constant state of "oneness" with Him in everything we do, in everything we think or feel, and indeed—in everything we are. Our walk is His walk. We are His agent and ambassador on this earth.

Through our actions, we sometimes make great efforts to have quiet time with God when we pray; and to approach Him with humility, submission, and awe. We do this oftentimes by going off by ourselves, kneeling down, closing our eyes, folding our hands a certain way, bowing our heads and beginning our prayer to Him.

If this helps us to tap into a sense of spirituality within ourselves that's great. However, if we live with a limiting mindset that says certain conditions must exist before we can properly communicate with God, we are limiting His ability to touch our lives in all that we think, do and are. We are denying the fact that, as Christians, God always lives inside us through his Holy Spirit regardless of our actions, thoughts, feelings, personality flaws, or in the mistakes and sins we make.

John 15:7 tells us if we are asking things of God (through our prayer life) <u>that are consistent with His perfect will for us</u>, we will receive them, and they will be done unto us. We are to ask God for things in our prayers but more importantly, we first pray for our own clarity in desiring what His will is for our life and the situation we are praying about. In this light and praying within this intended will for us, I Thessalonians 5:17 tells us that we should pray without ceasing. We should have faith through our prayers that God will answer what we ask for if, and only if, it is within His will (which He knows but we do not always).

We are given the greatest commandment in the New Covenant under Christ, which is stated in the 13th chapter of John. It tells us to love one another with all our hearts and our minds – and assumes we already have Christ in our hearts as our Savior. It goes beyond the Golden Rule to "do unto others as you would have them do unto you". The Platinum Rule says that we are to "do unto others as <u>they</u> would have us do unto them". Essentially, I may treat someone the way I would like to be treated. Or I may give them something that I may appreciate and value. But the other person might not want to be treated that way or value the same things we do. Good intentions are not always enough. So, it is important for us to take the time to find out just what form that love should take as we demonstrate it to others, and this only happens through sensitivity, communication, and empathy. This is an important dynamic of agape love. I write this to in no way say I am an expert. I am on the potter's wheel just like you.

I John 3:22 tells us that whatever we ask, we receive from Him, because we keep his commandment, and we are to do those things that are pleasing to Him. This means that, if we are truly demonstrating love for others by allowing the Holy Spirit to work in our lives, and if our purpose is to honor others through this selfless love, our prayers will reflect this.

I John 5:14-15 tells us that what we asked for in our prayers must be according to His will or these prayers will not be answered. Matthew 21:22 states we must wholeheartedly believe and have faith in God's ability to provide for us as well as in the saving grace of His Son's death and sacrifice on the Cross. It's almost as if we are to first pray for what we should pray for. In other words, to be able to calmy reflect and mediate with a sense of spiritual self-presence what it is in the situation that God wants us to be thankful or to ask for, with it always being according to his will.

We are told in Matthew that God takes care of all the needs of even the birds in the air and the lilies of the field and that they should not worry. God certainly cares more about us than He does birds and lilies and if all of their needs are taken care of, it is certain He will then take care of ours. As Christians, if we have the faith that God wants us to have, we realize this already and are fully trust that if we do not receive things in this life that we have prayed for, God did not intend for us to have them. These verses further state that, as we seek first the kingdom of God and understand more fully what God's will is for us, other things in our lives we think we need will not be as important to us; and perhaps we will no longer perceive them as needs - but instead, only as wants. Additionally, James 4:3 tells us that, if we are living our lives in His will for us, our prayers will be answered if we do not ask for things that are outside of that will.

The question can be asked about each of our Christian walks: "What are our needs and what are our wants?" Do we sometimes wholeheartedly believe what we need is only something we may just want based on carnal or 'in the moment' desires (probably driven by our sin nature)? If we completely believe one of God's most important precepts, that we should live our lives believing that He will always fulfill our every need, then why should we ever worry about being in need? And if we truly believe that God will take care of our every need and always knows what is best for us, why would we ever ask Him to work miracles in people's lives without having a full assurance that no matter how he answers our prayer, it will be within His best will for us and consistent with taking care of our every need? These kinds of questions lead us to ask another important one: If we do not pray, will God take care of our every need? The answer to this question is "of course". This does not mean however that we should be complacent in praying to God, in being in constant conversation with Him, and in humbling ourselves to allow the Holy Spirit to dominate all aspects of our life – because we certainly should. We should not have a mindset with God that says our prayers will cause Him to do something that is outside His perfect will for us, based on how hard we pray, or how many people we get to pray with us.

When we pray, we can ask for things from God but we do not cause or influence Him to do anything. We ask God for things but we preface these requests by telling Him first that our primary concern and desire is that we fully accept and trust in what His will is for our lives or for the situation; whether He answers our prayer in the affirmative or the negative. In God's omnipotent sovereignty, He already knows what will happen throughout all of eternity in every situation, and in all requests, petitions and praises we are going to direct His way. From this context, prayer is like getting a letter in the mail concerning a job offer that one has been waiting on for months. Just prior to opening the letter, the person can pray all he/she wants as to the job being offered, however, that prayer will not change what is already inside the letter - which has already been written days or even weeks earlier. Metaphorically, God knows the contents of the letter but we do not. Through prayer, we can ask for things but we realize and accept that, prior to our prayers and requests, God already knows what is going to happen. The part of the equation that is not known is that we do not know what is going to happen. Our prayers then are more for us to understand, be at peace, calm us, and accept God's will then they are for us to have God do what we want Him to do. This is sometimes hard for us to accept, especially when we are dealing with tragic events in our lives where we want to believe that a just and fair God would do what we ask in our dire times of need and respond to our humble requests (if we pray enough or ask Him in the right way). We can ask things of God in our prayers, but He is already aware of the outcome of the situation prior to our prayers to Him. Or stated more accurately, well before the situation ever arose, God was aware of it, knew how you were going to respond through your actions and prayer, took that into consideration, and set things in motion which would occur based on His perfect will.

Additionally, our own silent private prayers when no one is around, in and of themselves and separate from a change in our actions, do not influence what others will or won't do. This does not occur unless we communicate with others what those prayers are or change our heart based on the humility we experience in conversation with God. All too often, we pray for things we need in the privacy of our own homes or separate from others, but we never ask another person to help, or we don't turn our prayer into actions and step into to help another person who is the object of that prayer. All too often, we fail to bring out humility in ourselves and ask for help or assistance from others due to our pride. This has to change if we are to live out a full and complete Christian life where we are not only blessings to others as we help them out but simultaneously, we are blessings to them because we allow them to help us out.

Many churches have "Prayer Chains" where someone finds out about a health issue or a need of an individual and shares it in some way for everyone to pray about. This is a wonderful thing, if and only if people in the 'prayer chain' do something other than just pray about the need or situation. In other words, where they engage and somehow fill a need by reaching out to the person offering encouragement, making a meal, or volunteering to take them to a doctor's appointment. All too often, we just offer people or a situation our thoughts and prayers and then stop there. Grace and our Christian walk require more.

Also, and I think this is truer of men than women, we have so much pride that we do not humble ourselves and ask when we need help with something. It's almost as if we are saying that I will help out when someone else is in need but I will never allow myself to be vulnerable, in need, and ask for help myself.

Sometimes the 'prayer chain' (with great intention) jumps into action and tells everyone what they should be praying for instead of instructing everyone to first pray for God's will in the situation. The prayer chain may automatically ask for prayers for someone to come home from the hospital as quickly as possible. But what if God wanted that person to stay there one more day to witness to the doctors and nurses?

Our faith, as demonstrated somewhat by our prayer life, does not move mountains, as has been misunderstood in the reading of Scripture. The tremendous faith we have, as demonstrated through our prayers, acts as only a vehicle for our acceptance of what God's predestination and action is for our lives. The mountain that is moved is our perspective and attitude change of the situation , and His determination to create greater spiritual resiliency in each of us. In this context, if our needs are not taken care of by God, this means that He does not define them as needs. II Corinthians 9:8 states that: "God is able to make all Grace abound toward you; that you, <u>always having all sufficiency in all things</u> may abound to every good work." As believer Christians, we know that Christ lives within us and His Holy Spirit is constantly guiding us to help us live in the faith of Christ who gave Himself for us (Gal. 2:20).

Matthew 11:25-26 and Luke 10:21 tell us the importance of our prayers constantly giving praise to God for the things He has blessed us with and how we should be thankful for them. Luke 18:13 tells us that we should pray to be thankful for the mercy that God bestows on us. Luke 23:34 tells us to pray to God for Him to help us open our hearts further and use what He has already given to us through His mercy by continually forgiving our enemies and to help us in our spiritual strength throughout our Christian walk.

When we pray it is important that we approach God in humility. <u>Our prayers should focus on ourselves and others to grow in understanding God's grace that He has already blessed us with; and for us to use and benefit from this grace.</u> When we see the faults in others and observe their sins, we fully understand we are just as guilty of sins in our own lives (probably more so) than the individual we are observing or judging. We should not compare our Christian walk with how well others are able to be in theirs. This is something I have struggled with for years. We should only be concerned with ourselves and our relationship with God and how well we are able to use the gifts and talents that He has given to us. Matthew 7:7 tells us we should ask, and it should be given unto us; that we should seek, and we shall find; and we should knock and the door shall be opened unto us. This verse only applies if our prayers, and the things that we ask for, are within God's will. If those prayers are consistent with God's perfect will for us, they will certainly move mountains. As stated above, the moving of those mountains however may take the form of helping us change our internal attitudes about something that God is trying to convict us of and work on our hearts. God knows what it is best for our lives. Even if we do not understand for the short-term, God understands what is best for us in the long-term.

Faith is that spiritual element we have that not only brings us to God but also helps us understand and accept His plan for us. Through our patience, we can see with clearer understanding, what our best life can be within the will of God. In His Word, God provides us encouragement and a demonstration of the support He gives us in many areas of our lives. In times of loneliness, Hebrews 13:5-6 and Isaiah 41:10 tell us that we should be content with the things that we have and that He will never leave us or forsake us. In turmoil, God tells us (in Philippians 4:6-7) that in everything, through prayer and supplication with thanksgiving, we should let all our requests be known to Him (which will only be granted if they are in line with Gods perfect will for us and where God sees them as our needs.) With the peace of God, which passes all understanding, we will be comforted in our hearts and minds through Christ. When we have sorrow in our lives, Romans 8:26,28 tells us the Holy Spirit will help us know what we should pray for and that all things work together for good to them that love God, to them who are called according to His purpose. This is also reflected in II Corinthians 1:3-5. In times of suffering, God gives us the comfort of the words in Hebrews 12:3-13 where it states that whom the Lord loves he disciplines (teaches and guides) and if we endure this chastening, we become as His sons (as any loving father would discipline their own son).

These verses also tell us that as we are going through trials and tribulations, we do not understand the profit or potential for growth in it at the time, but after it is over, we are able to look back in great introspection and spiritual wisdom and appreciate what we have learned - and the knowledge and temperance we now have since we are on the other side of that obstacle or event. Many unbelievers unfortunately reject this concept but then readily accept the worldly interpretation of this same principle as being true: "There are no problems, only opportunities", and "when you're give lemons, make lemonade".

In times of indecision, Proverbs 3:5-6 and James 1:5-6 provide us with tremendous spiritual focus. In times of fear, we have the confident words found in Ephesians 6:10-18 and Hebrews 13:5-6 which provide calm to us. In times of weariness, we have Matthew 11 and Psalm 23 which gives us confidence to go forward. <u>As we pray and meditate with God, He shows us the</u>

<u>great peace which he has already provided us with through His Holy Spirit as we more fully understand the depths of His grace.</u> Prayer can give us tremendous understanding as to situations that other people are dealing with as well; and in the process, helps us to deal with them more effectively from a spiritual perspective. Prayer helps to give us wisdom as to understanding God's purpose for our lives and not only showing love to others, but also in showing us how to give love to others. Prayer can sometimes act as a mirror by reflecting to us how we are coming across to others as we live out our Christian walk.

We also may not immediately understand God's purpose in answering our prayers the way He does however, there is a purpose, and it is the best for our life. God looks at life from an eternal standpoint and not as a limited continuum of time the way we as humans see it; limited to the time in this world. God has a more long-term plan for us which transcends our physical world and enters spiritual eternity. The 40th chapter of Isaiah outlines God's greatness and our weakness and limitations in our capacity to understand truths. God's greatness is demonstrated as He Himself became flesh in the person of Christ and was able to demonstrate pure (agape) love - as outlined in I Corinthians 13. The greatness of God is also demonstrated in His plan of salvation and a new birth for us which is outlined in John 3. As stated in II Corinthians 6:14-7:1, prayer helps us to be separated from worldliness and understand our role, with a clearer perspective, in terms of us being in the world; but not necessarily of the world. As we continue to grow in grace, prayer provides us with important heavenly wisdom from God through His Son and Holy Spirit (James 3:14-18).

James 5:15-16 and Matthew 9:38 tell us we should pray for others so that they may become saved. This is more for us to prepare our own hearts as we witness and show example to others. The only thing that a Christian will not be able to do in Heaven in the next life (that they can do here on this earth) is to lead others to Christ and offer them the opportunity for eternal life. I Peter 4:7

tells us that we are to arm ourselves with prayer through continual spiritual contact with God. Through this contact, we become greater vehicles and ambassadors in representing the gospel to others. Through our prayer, we understand greater spiritual knowledge and judgment so we can provide love to others more in the manner that God would have us (Philippians 1:9).

The world gives us temptation in many areas of our lives as we live out our Christian walk with God. God provides peaceful guidance and instruction as to how best to handle this temptation (Mark 14:38 and Luke 22:46). Job 22:27, 33:26, and Psalm 6:9 assure us we should have total confidence that God will answer our prayers if they are in His will for us and others. I Corinthians 7:5 encourages us to re-approach situations with new wisdom through prayer after we have had difficulties with those issues in the past. We can also pray or meditate (reflect) to fully understand God's grace and wisdom on how to handle weaker Christians and provide encouragement to them (I Peter 3:7). This is not wisdom received from God as the result of prayer however, it is tapping into spiritual wisdom and grace that God has already given to us at the time of our salvation and tapping into the limitless Holy Spirit which resides in us. He is not giving us anything new as much as He is helping us to understand more fully what has already been given to us. Lastly, God has tremendous contempt for hypocrites and those who pray publicly in order that others may view them as being holier (than others) while acting as though they have greater and more intimate spiritual contact with God because of who they are (Matthew 6:5, 7, 9; 23:14) and how their actions are seen by others.

Reflection & Study Questions For This Chapter:

- How do you define prayer? What is it, and what is it not?

- Do you believe God always answers prayer?

- Before we ask God for anything in our prayers, what is the most important thing we should pray for?

- Do you believe your prayers cause God to do things?

- Do you believe God grants requests in your prayers when they may not be part of His will?

- Do you believe God takes of your needs, without you always praying for them?

- Think of a time when you prayed for something and it didn't happen or turn out the way you wanted it to. How did it turn out in the end? Was it a blessing that you did not get what you prayed for? What did you learn from that situation?

Chapter 8

The Anointed Cherub and Worldliness

Writing about the Christian walk and the grace message would not be complete without discussing the challenges and obstacles in a believers way in this world as they try to demonstrate love as outlined in I Corinthians and the fruits of the Spirit in Galatians 5 and 6. There is so much evil in the world each of us face on a daily basis from those who misuse power, to political distortion and corruption, senseless wars, child abuse, human trafficking, unfair immigration policies, racism, gun violence, apostacy that is taught in our churches, and the list goes on. It is important for each of us to understand where much of this evil originates from and the dynamics surrounding it. To credit a sovereign God, each of us are created as free moral agents to choose different paths in our lives based on our own free will. We can choose good over evil, positive over negative, and the path of the Holy Spirit over the evil that is in this world.

The Bible states that God created Satan as the most beautiful angel for many reasons, one of which was to orchestrate praises and glory to Him. Through time, Satan believed he was just like God and deserved the same praise and glory He had so he became rebellious and began soliciting followers to worship him. Satan (also referred to as the Devil and Lucifer) is the oppressor of man (II Timothy 2:26, Psalm 107:2, Ephesians 2:2, and II Corinthians 4:4). One objective of Satan is to prevent Christians from serving the Lord based on the special gifts God has given each one. He does this by sidetracking and distracting us with things that look beautiful or seem good to us. This is not hard for Satan to do since he was created as one of the most, if not the most beautiful, creatures in the world. Therefore, Satan is fully aware of not only what is beautiful and appealing to mankind in general but also specifically, what is most appealing and inviting to each of us individually; in essence what each one of our weaknesses and vulnerabilities are that can be exploited; like finding the weakest link in a chain. This is extremely important to understand and has huge effects since each one of us have extremely vulnerable areas that can be exploited differently than other Christians.

Using a metaphor from fishing, experienced fisherman know there are certain kinds of lures that should be used if you're going to catch different kinds of fish, under different kinds of conditions. Satan understands we are all different as individuals and unique and therefore must use different lures to tempt us; essentially, different things in this world which have the greatest impact on us individually as temptation.

The creation of Satan, as outlined in Ezekial 28, tells us he was given a covering of special stones such as topaz, diamonds, beryl, onyx, jasper, sapphires, emeralds, carbuncle, and gold. God created Satan as being wiser than even Daniel; and no secret was hidden from him. He was created as being full of wisdom and perfect in beauty with a wingspan larger than all other angels. Ezekial 28 states that Satan's heart was filled with pride because of his great beauty and wisdom and therefore he was corrupted through "reason of thy brightness". This is an amazing way that Scripture expresses the character of pride. Satan defiled the attributes given to him with lust for gain. Satan eventually began believing he was God and set his heart as that of the heart of God. He used wisdom and understanding to gain great wealth and his heart was lifted to these riches.

Because Satan was created with such beauty and wisdom, it is not difficult for him to tempt us with beautiful things that are appealing to us. Satan is an expert at deception and at <u>giving good things to people to keep them from the best things that God has planned for them.</u> Satan will get us involved in many good things such as social issues, education, those who are homeless, world hunger, deaconship, the abortion issue, and many others -

in order that we would be distracted at following God's perfect will for our lives and us obtaining the best things; such as in the area of powerful personal ministries which may be different than those mentioned above. II Corinthians 11:14 tells us that Satan is transformed into an angel of light and therefore it is easier for him to deceive us.

Satan also uses sidetracking attitudes to distract us from doing the most important things we should be doing. As born-again believers, this takes the form of witnessing to others who may not be saved through our words and/or our example; the only thing we can do on this earth that we won't be able to do in Heaven. One of the tactics used by Satan to accomplish his goals is to confuse us from understanding truth. The book of I Corinthians tells us that God is not the author of confusion and John 14:6 tells us that Jesus is the Truth. In contrast, Satan is very efficient in confusing us through false doctrines and derailing our ability to make choices that reflect us being indwelt with the Holy Spirit.

Whatever it takes for us to be stopped in accomplishing God's will for our lives is what Satan will put it in our way. Satan's opposition to God and man is clearly seen in Scripture:

- He leads men to steal from God (Acts 5:3).
- He works primarily as an entity which is disobedient to God (Ephesians 2:2).
- He tempts married couples sexually (I Corinthians 7:5).
- He lies and is the father of lies (John 8:44).
- He causes murder and killing (John 8:44 and I John 3:12).
- He snatches the Word out of man's heart (Matthew 13:19).
- He plants unbelievers in the midst of believers to negatively influence their walk (Matthew 13:38,39).
- He launches powerful strategies against believers (Ephesians 6:11).
- He rules the principalities and powers, the darkness and spiritual wickedness of this world (Ephesians 6:12; Colossians 2:15).

- He hinders the work of believers (I Thes. 2:18).
- He leads men to blaspheme (I Timothy 1:20).
- He transforms some unbelievers into ministers of righteousness to deceive men (II Corinthians 11:15).
- He transforms himself into a messenger of light to deceive men (II Corinthians 11:14).
- He deceives the minds of men (II Corinthians 11:3).
- He blinds the mind of unbelievers to prevent them from believing in God (II Corinthians 4:4).
- He tries hard to keep people from forgiving others (II Corinthians 2:10, 11).
- He turns people aside and distracts them from following him (I Timothy 5:15).
- He sins and works against God and men (I John 3:8).
- He deceives the whole world (Revelation 12:9; 3:9).

Looking at these versus in their totality, we get a better picture as to the power and influence the works of Satan can have in our lives; possibly without us even fully realizing it. Additionally, Satan uses the natural forces existing in the world to assist him in accomplishing the objectives of his agenda. As an example, many aspects of secular psychology tell us that we are mini-gods, that we have the capacity within ourselves (without God) to become spiritually complete and to become present and self-actualized, and that we should do what feels good to insure we constantly have a positive self-concept.

In this author's opinion, of all aspects of God's creation, the human mind and heart is His greatest. Therefore, the field of psychology is a viable endeavor (consistent with God's principles) as long as it maintains its proper focus and perspective, which is that all aspects of the human mind and heart have been created by Him and should be used for His glory and that we are completely dependent on Him. All of these amazing psychological dynamics have been created by God.

Although the word "Daimonia" in the Greek is generally translated "devil", the correct word is actually "demon" (Satan). As to the reality and personality of demons, the New Testament scripture brings out great testimony as to their origin and character. The Old Covenant tells us that Demons are spirits (Matthew 12:43-45) and are Satan's emissaries (Matthew 12:26, 27.) Demons know that Christ is the most high God and recognize His supreme authority (Matthew 8:31-32; Mark 1:23-24; Acts 19:15 and James 2:19). Demons know their eternal fate is being one of torment (Matthew 8:29 and Luke 8:31) and that their nature is to maintain a conflict with Christians who otherwise would be more spiritual in their lives on this earth (Ephesians 6:12; I Timothy 4:1-3).

One responsibility of the believer is to witness to non-believers so they can experience the gifts of the Holy Spirit through their salvation. Therefore, it is important for believers to be aware of some of methods Satan uses to keep non-believers from accepting Christ into their lives. In terms of salvation of the unbeliever, Satan uses at least three methods to keep people from being saved according to God's word in scripture: prevention, distortion, and procrastination. Prevention refers to Satan's ability to stop people from attending church and creating distractions in their lives so that they will not hear, listen to, or fully understand the gospel message (I Corinthians 1:18; Romans 10:17; I Corinthians 1:21). Distortion refers to Satan's ability to distort God's truth to be applied in our lives. Satan is an expert at deception and distortion and at perverting people's understanding (II Corinthians 4:4; Luke 8:12). Procrastination refers to Satan's ability to create conditions which make it easy for us to put things off for as long as we can. Usually, after much time has elapsed, the job or action either never gets done or when it is finally completed, its impact is reduced.

In terms of Satan's relationship with believers, his agenda and primary objective for those who already know Christ as their Savior is to: stop evangelism, ruin Christian testimonies, keep us from growing, and keep us from serving God as completely as we should. It is interesting to know that the first time God mentions His church in the New Testament is in the context of spiritual warfare. When we speak of Satan's desire to stop evangelism, we understand this to mean Satan does not want others to be saved into God's church (II Corinthians 2:11; Matthew 16:13,21; I Thessalonians 2:4). Satan's ongoing and clear attempts to ruin our testimony is stated in I Peter 5:8 and Psalm 51. Satan keeps us from growing by distracting us with noble things (and things that are full of pleasure), by keeping us away from church (Luke 10:38; Ephesians 4:15; I Peter 2:2), and by distracting us from prayer and our Christian growth. Satan also keeps us from fully serving Christ as is stated in II Peter 3:18 and I Peter 2:2.

Romans 6:16 tells us we freely choose our master: either Satan as our god resulting in sin and death; or God as our Master resulting in eternal joy and everlasting life through our spiritual salvation. Luke 22:31 and II Timothy 3:1-5 states that Satan wants to govern our lives and sift us as a farmer sifts wheat. However, Satan has already been defeated and "we are more than conquerors through Him that loved us" (Romans 8:37). We can have real security knowing we are born-again believers assured of a place in Heaven. Our job, as Christians, is to submit to the Holy Spirit in our lives and allow it to work in us according to the perfect will of God with Christ as our loving model as example.

John 15:19 tells us that Christians are supposed to be in the world, but not of the world. In Isaiah 52:11, believers are said to touch not the unclean thing and to go out from among those who do, thus separating themselves. In II Corinthians 6:17, Christians are expected to come out from among them and to "be separate from the world". God has always wanted prudent separation of the righteous from the unrighteous, believers from un-believers – so that the lifestyles of the un-believer would not interfere and distract the believer from living out a more full and complete life based on God's will for them. What this looks like in day-to-day living is that dedicated and continued fellowship with non-believers is dangerous and could significantly impact the believer's walk. Christians should not intermingle with other Christians who are continuously engaged in an unhealthy impure lifestyle (I Corinthians 5: 9-13). Doing so may interfere with their walk with God and stagnate their testimony and the striving for purity and progress towards increased growth in Grace. Ephesians 5:11 states that Christians are not to have continued fellowship with the unfruitful works of darkness.

With all this said, it is critical for the Christian to not take a reclusive position in their walk on this earth. If one of our main goals is to help others know the saving grace of God, and we never allow ourselves to be out in the "real world" exposing ourselves to un-believers (constantly maintaining a sterile separation from all others), how are others supposed to hear the Gospel and the love of the Holy Spirit; which many times can only be seen by the un-believer in our actions as Christians? These are not the actions of the Holy Spirit if we stay so insulated from the world that we focus on maintaining our spiritual security and pureness at the expense of leading others to Christ because we fear our testimony may be injured in some way. At some point, this becomes selfish and self-centered on our part and contrary to the spiritual nature and challenge within us. This is a tremendous challenge to each believer in terms of finding that <u>balance</u> between spending time with non-believers to witness to them and be a Christian example (showing our light among darkness) - with the responsibility we must be separate from the world and not allow our own Christian walk to be interfered with. Fortunately, each one has their own calling and special gifts that equip them to rise to that calling. Each one must decide in their own heart, under the guidance of the Holy Spirit, where that line is and how best they can maximize the tremendous opportunities that God sets before each of us.

George Elliot once said that "It's never too late to be what you might have been." There is nothing we can do about time that has gone by and what is in the past. There is much we can do about the present and the future that awaits each person, and to live into God's potential for us. We each have been created as free moral agents with tremendous gifts, talents, and capacities. We are empowered to make our own deliberate and intentional choices to influence this world, and those in it who are put in front of us, according to our spiritual, emotional, intellectual, and physical blessings. As we go through the different seasons of our lives and our own unique process of Christian sanctification where we progressively are more able to allow the Holy Spirit to freely work through us unencumbered by our carnal worldly selves, our capacity to demonstrate grace is slowly perfected. Essentially, a journey through our personal and spiritual blessings, challenges, trails and tribulations; all of our different seasons of grace perfection.

With tremendous wisdom, and as a believer, Marianne Williamson tells us that "Our deepest fear is not that we are inadequate. It is that we are powerful beyond measure. We ask ourselves: Who am I to be brilliant, gorgeous, talented, and fabulous. Actually, who are you not to be? Your playing small does not serve the world. There is nothing enlightened about shrinking so that others around you won't feel insecure. We are all meant to shine our light, as children do. We were born to make manifest the glory of God that is in each one of us. And as we let our own light shine, we unconsciously give other people permission to do the same."

Reflection & Study Questions For This Chapter:

- Are you sometimes engaged in good things that keep you from engaging in the best things for your life?

- What is the payoff for you focusing on the good things in your life when you could be engaged in the best things?

- Phillipeans 4:13 says we can do all things through Christ. God is not a God of fear but peace, security, and ability. What would you do in your life if you were not afraid? What steps could you take to begin moving in that direction?

www.ingramcontent.com/pod-product-compliance
Lightning Source LLC
Chambersburg PA
CBHW051216290426
44109CB00021B/2477